KOLYMA

KOLYMA

The Arctic Death Camps

ROBERT CONQUEST

THE VIKING PRESS
New York

For
KINGSLEY and JANE AMIS

Published in 1978 by The Viking Press
625 Madison Avenue, New York, N.Y. 10022

LIBRARY OF CONGRESS CATALOGING IN PUBLICATION DATA
Conquest, Robert.
Kolyma.
Bibliography: p.
Includes index.
1. Kolyma, Siberia.   2.   Penal colonies, Russian.
3.   Political prisoners—Russia.   I.   Title.
HV8964.R8C66   365'.3   77-26274
ISBN 0-670-41499-9

Printed in the United States of America
Set in Baskerville

Grateful acknowledgement is made to the following for permission to use material:

Europa Verlag AG: From *Eleven Years in Soviet Prison Camps* by Elinor Lipper.

Harcourt Brace Jovanovich, Inc.: From *Journey into the Whirlwind* by Eugenia Semyonovna Ginzburg, Copyright © 1967 by Arnoldo Mondadori Editore—Milano; English translation Copyright © 1967 by Harcourt Brace Jovanovich, Inc. Reprinted by permission of Harcourt Brace Jovanovich, Inc.

CONTENTS

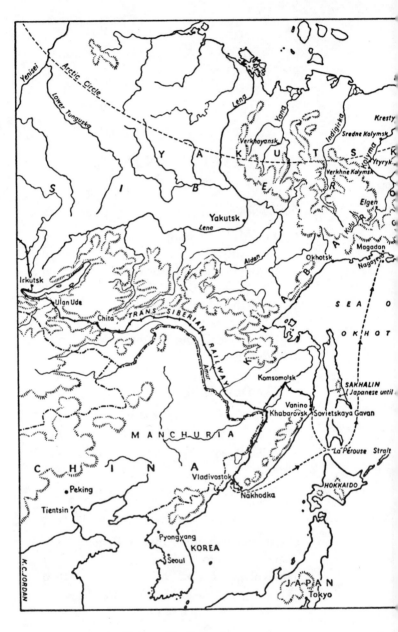

USSR showing the Kolyma Region and sea routes

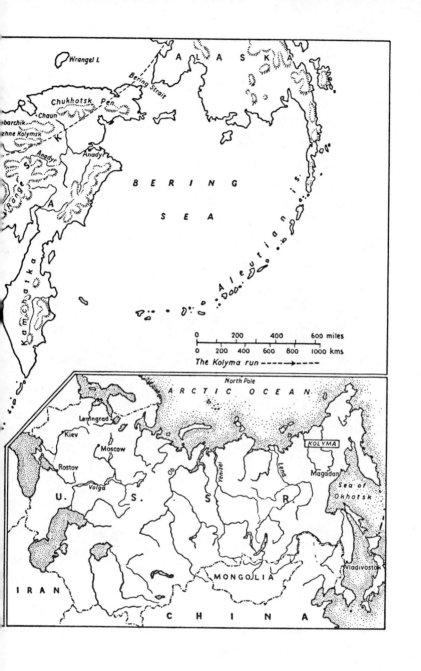

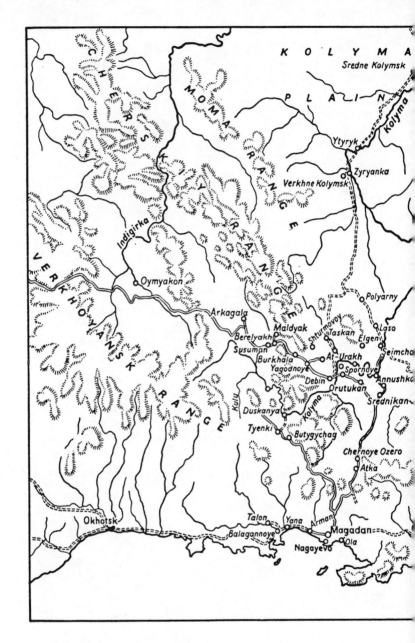

Kolyma Region

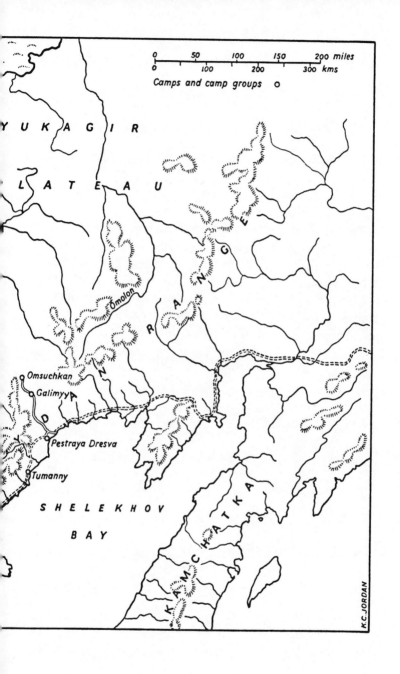

ACKNOWLEDGEMENTS

Acknowledgements are due to the sources quoted in the text, mainly ex-prisoners, and in particular to Vladimir Petrov, Elinor Lipper, Michael Solomon and the late Varlam Shalamov; and also to Lloyd's of London, who helped me with their records; to Anna Bourguina of the Hoover Institution, Stanford; and to Marie Collett, for her invaluable assistance in preparing the material.

INTRODUCTION

THE present work is a documentation from a number of sources, both Soviet and Western, in which I seek to establish beyond cavil the history and the conditions of the huge labour camp complex of Kolyma.*

Kolyma constitutes, it is true, only one section of the 'Archipelago' (as Solzhenitsyn has so aptly named it) of the NKVD's penal empire, scattered throughout the vast territories of the Soviet North and East. But, just as Auschwitz has come to stand for the Nazi extermination camps as a whole, so Kolyma remains fixed in the imagination of the Soviet peoples as the great archetype of the sinister system under which Stalin ended, by hunger, cold and exhaustion, the lives of so many of his subjects. (It was natural, during a celebrated debate among Soviet historians in the early sixties, that when Dr A. V. Snegov was denouncing the Stalin heritage and was pressed by the Stalinist historian Deborin to say did he belong to the Soviet or the anti-Soviet camp, he should have retorted, 'I belong to the Kolyma Camp.')

The sinister reputation of the Kolyma camps is, of course, primarily due to the fact that, of the mass-imprisonment areas at least, it was the deadliest. There seem, indeed, to have been camps on the Arctic islands of Novaya Zemlya from which no one returned at all: but of these practically

*The accent falls on the last syllable.

13

nothing is known, and they were certainly on a smaller scale. In Kolyma, millions died: and it is possible, owing to the special circumstances of the area, to obtain reasonable estimates of the numbers. The point here is that Kolyma was supplied by sea; and we have some knowledge of the number of ships in service, their capacity, and the number of trips they made a year.

This isolation from the 'mainland', as the prisoners always referred to it, coupled with the fact that the area is in the furthest corner of the enormous Soviet territory, contributed greatly to the prisoners' feeling of having been removed irrevocably from the normal world—an effect especially powerful for inhabitants of the great land mass. It also produced characteristics hardly to be found in the rest of the Archipelago (for example that precautions against escape were less thorough, since escape in any real sense was virtually impossible).

It thus seems not only comparatively simple to treat this separate area in isolation, but also peculiarly appropriate to do so: particularly as Solzhenitsyn himself, though he gives us a few illuminating pages on the area, says in *The Gulag Archipelago*, 'I have almost excluded Kolyma from the compass of this book.'

As he notes, there are several accounts of Kolyma by Soviet writers—as well as others, which he did not know of at the time, by former inmates in the West. What I have done, in effect, is to bring these accounts together on a reasonably systematic basis, to give as full and irrefutable a picture as possible of this dreadful monument to in-humanity.

I have relied basically on seventeen main first-hand accounts—sixteen from ex-prisoners, and one from a free employee. In addition, I have used a few major reports and analyses published in the West or in the Soviet press, together with some hitherto unpublished information.

Of the major first-hand accounts, twelve were provided by witnesses who had reached the West, and five by witnesses remaining in the Soviet Union. Of the latter, two were actually published in Moscow, and two others, though originally intended for Soviet publication, were finally refused this and were later published in the West; but none of the writers were prosecuted for their revelations.

Ten of these testimonies are from present or former Soviet citizens; four from Poles; one from a Romanian, one from a Swiss, and one from a German. Thirteen are from men and four from women—two of the latter among the most valuable.

And, in addition to these, I have relied to a lesser extent on half a dozen unpublished witnesses, former victims, whose testimony is summarised by Roy Medvedev in *Let History Judge*, by Dallin and Nicolaevsky in *Forced Labour in Soviet Russia*, by Solzhenitsyn in *The Gulag Archipelago*, and elsewhere; as well as by the evidence, based on the affidavits of 63 Polish prisoners, summarised in Silvester Mora's booklet *Kolyma*.

The experience of these men and women extends from the earliest beginnings of Kolyma, in 1932 to 1933, to the rehabilitations which started to take place in 1954. And their broad range of background and experience seems more than adequate to provide a clear, full and irrefutable picture of Kolyma.

It has often been pointed out that while Auschwitz and Maidanek are known the world over, the Soviet equivalents are not. Since the publication of *The Gulag Archipelago*, the existence and nature of the Soviet camp system in general has penetrated the world's consciousness. But, except in the Soviet Union itself, this has been as a system and far less as a local habitation and a name. For Russians—and it is surely right that this should become true for the world as a whole—Kolyma is a word of horror wholly comparable to Auschwitz. And the first and easiest point to remember is that it did indeed kill some three million people, a figure well in the range of that of the victims of the Final Solution.

It is not my purpose to argue whether Stalin's mass murders were worse than Hitler's or vice versa. Both were on a horrible scale and both were conducted with such inhumanity that such comparisons seem otiose. We may, indeed, note certain differences. Hitler's atrocities were carried out against those he had himself declared to be his enemies. Stalin's were a random operation against his own subjects and supporters. Stalin, simply because he had a longer period to operate in and a larger pool of potential victims, killed a good many more than Hitler did. A final difference is, of course, that Stalin found defenders among sensitive-minded liberals in the West and Hitler did not. Moreover Stalin's terror was one of the foundation stones of a system which, far from being part of history, flourishes to this day. The resources of Kolyma, so long developed at the expense of prisoners' lives, are now largely exploited by free labour backed by adequate machinery. But its name remains in the Russian mind as epitomising more than any other the horrors of the Stalin era. Nor has the change been complete. There are still labour camps in Kolyma, as elsewhere in Russia: in 1971 Andrei Amalrik was sent to serve out a sentence in a strict-regime camp in the area, for the crime of spreading 'falsehoods against the Soviet state and the system'. These were, of course, nothing of the kind, but merely expressions of opinions or statements of fact unwelcome to the KGB. For the Secret Police still exists and still administers—even if on a smaller scale—the Gulag Archipelago of which Kolyma, beyond the icy waters of the Okhotsk Sea, was the most dreadful and distant island.

The way in which the memory of Kolyma still haunts the Soviet present may be seen in a case which came particularly vividly to public notice in 1976, with the publication in the West of the autobiography of Georgi Vins, the Soviet Reform Baptist leader, under the significant title *Three Generations of Suffering*. Pastor Vins, who had himself already been imprisoned for his religious activities (and was to be again after publication of the book), deals with the earlier sufferings of his father in the same cause, which ended with death in Kolyma in December 1943.

Basically, the frightfulness of Kolyma was due not to geographical or climatic reasons, but to conscious decisions taken in Moscow. For a few years before 1937, in fact, it was well administered and the death rate was low. The climate, though exceedingly cold, is a remarkably healthy one for men who are properly fed, clothed and sheltered. In this earlier phase, the main aim of the administration was to produce gold efficiently. In the later period (as one commandant put it quite openly) though the gold remained important, the central aim was to kill off the prisoners. In the earliest period of the labour camp system, the Solovki camps on the islands of the White Sea were the symbol of the whole system, the worst killers. These were followed, in the mid-thirties, by the camps of the Baltic – White Sea Canal. Kolyma took their place just when the system was reaching its maximum expansion, and remained central to it for the next fifteen years, as (in Solzhenitsyn's words) 'the pole of cold and cruelty' of the labour camp system.

CHAPTER ONE

THE MIDDLE PASSAGE

Death-ships of the Okhotsk Sea . . .
ANDREI SAKHAROV

WE take up the story of the endless stream of victims as they arrive on the Soviet Pacific shore, on the seas beyond which lay their eventual destination—Kolyma's port of Naga-yevo, its central staging area at Magadan, and behind them the camps and mines of the interior.

For readers will be familiar with the earlier stages in the sufferings of the victim of the Great Purge. From his night-time arrest; his life in the incredibly overcrowded cells of the Butyrka or the Lefortovo, or the Lubyanka, or Leningrad's Kresty or Shlaperny prisons, or in one of the hundreds of prisons of the lesser cities; the interrogation, at which confession to an entirely false charge was obtained by the continuous questioning without sleep of the 'conveyor' or by physical torture; then the days or weeks in the crowded and lightless cattle truck of the prison train conveying him to his camp.

We will begin, then, with the prisoners arriving at the huge transit camps on the Pacific coast, outside Vladivostok and later at Nakhodka, and at Vanino, in each of which a hundred thousand prisoners would be crowded into the endless array of barracks which stretched as far as the eye could see. There they awaited the prison ships of the Kolyma run.

Those who arrived were already crushed and humiliated, starved and ill-clad remnants of human beings. They would normally have spent around three months in prison under conditions and treatment thought adequate to such as they. And the train journey—always one of the worst of the various experiences of the victims, with its fetid wagons, its inadequate water supply, its lack of food and light, its brutal guards—was, of course, the longest undergone by any of Gulag's victims: 28 days, 33 days, 35 days, 47 days are typical times reported.

On arrival they piled out of the train and were at once surrounded by guards with dogs. They would be told to squat and the guards would shout the routine warning, 'If anyone stands up we shall take it as an attempt to escape and shoot instantly.' —All quite normal.

After a checking of documents by the train guards and the camp guards, the consignment of prisoners would be marched off—to the transit camps.

These huge camps do not need to be described in great detail. Life in them resembled in most aspects the general camp life of the Archipelago. The differences were mainly in the absence of physical labour, and the knowledge of impermanence.

At the Vladivostok transit camp, in the thirties, there were two zones, one for common criminals and one for counter-revolutionaries. The former had heated barracks, blankets, mattresses and other luxuries not available at the latter. In the counter-revolutionary section, there was always a grave shortage of water, which produced fights. Still, this was better than the company of the criminals. When the Vladivostok camp was moved to Nakhodka at the beginning of the war, and the Vanino camp—much further north—later opened up, such segregation was no longer practised. The tough General Gorbatov was both cheated and violently robbed at Nakhodka. There was the usual despoilment of all possessions, including overcoats, by thieves at Vanino.

It is not certain when it was that Vanino, just north of Sovietskaya Gavan, became fully operational. Though nearer both to Central Russia and (by sea) to Nagayevo, it at first had no rail connection to the Trans-Siberian. There was a large camp in the area as early as 1940, though it is not clear whether this was already a main transit camp for Kolyma. (One of several reported strikes by Polish prisoners to secure delivery of their rations is reported there in that year, involving finally several thousand men, including Russians and others. It resulted in mass machine-gunning.)

At whichever camp, once settled in, prisoners tried to take advantage of the vast crowds to meet acquaintances. Everyone hoped to find husbands or other close relatives, but with a woman serving a sentence which took her to Kolyma, the husband had almost invariably been shot. One girl of Eugenia Ginzburg's group did meet her brother, who gave her a small pillow and blamed himself for her arrest. She later gave him the pillow back, as the only thing she had, before boarding the *Dzhurma*: he was shot in 1944 for anti-Soviet talk in camp, to be rehabilitated in the 1950s.[4]*

Many prisoners, of course, died in the transit camps. Those we know of include the Russian poet Osip Mandelstam and the Polish poet Bruno Jasienski. General Gorbatov tells of an old colleague:

I met Ushakov, former commander of the Ninth Division. We flung our arms around each other and, of course, wept. Ushakov had once been thought a man of culture, the best of the divisional commanders. Here he was a foreman in charge of nine camp kitchens, and still considered himself

*Superior figures refer to the Bibliography and References at p. 243.

21

fortunate to have such 'privileged' work. Ushakov never reached Kolyma, because of his health. An old soldier, he had been wounded eighteen times fighting the Basmachi in Central Asia. He had received four medals for his military service. While we were at Nakhodka Bay Ushakov's fate, for no apparent reason, took a turn for the worse; he was demoted from foreman and put on heavy physical labour.[5]

And so died.

Mrs Ginzburg describes the death of a friend, almost fleshless, blind and disfigured with scurvy, whom not even the bugs of the transit camp would approach. The bugs were so legendary, even by camp standards, that they are reported in almost all the prisoners' accounts as provoking every night a struggle which would last till dawn. As soon as it got barely warm enough, prisoners would move out of the barracks and sleep on the ground, only to be followed by a veritable 'procession of the virulent insects'. Lice too abounded. The disinfestation chambers worked inefficiently. A typhus epidemic, as a result, swept the camp in 1938 causing tens of thousands of deaths. Over the following year a new camp commandant finally improved the de-lousing system and brought the epidemic under control.

The survivors of this, and of mere starvation, would, when the time came, be checked for working capacity. At the Vanino camp in 1949, a regular slave market was in operation. Officials from various mining areas, accompanied by doctors, would examine the wares. One group is reported to have had a standing contract with the NKVD for 120,000 labourers a year. 'They felt men's muscles, opened their mouths to check their teeth and looked at eyes, head and shoulders.'[31] As elsewhere, the method of testing for dystrophy was to pinch the buttocks. If the muscle was still elastic the prisoner was judged as not in so advanced a condition as to be unfitted for hard labour.

Embarkation day would arrive. At Vanino:

When we came out on to the immense field outside the camp I witnessed a spectacle that would have done justice to a Cecil B. DeMille production. As far as the eye could see there were columns of prisoners marching in one direction or another like armies on a battlefield. A huge detachment of security officers, soldiers, and signal corpsmen with field telephones and motor-cycles kept in touch with headquarters, arranging the smooth flow of these human rivers. I asked what this giant operation was meant to be. The reply was that each time a transport was sent off the administration reshuffled the occupants of every cage in camp so that everyone had to be removed with his bundle of rags on his shoulder to the big field and from there directed to his new destination. Only 5000 were supposed to leave, but 100,000 were part of the scene before us. One could see endless columns of women, of cripples, of old men and even teenagers, all in military formation, five in a row, going through the huge field, and directed by whistles or flags. It was more than three hours before the operation was completed and the batch I belonged to was allowed to leave for the embarkation point.[31]

In these camps, depending on the time of year, a prisoner might be held for only a few days or—if he arrived after the end of the navigation season—from early December until late April. After the trains the camp, at any rate in summer and in the absence of epidemics, had afforded somewhat of a relief. It had been possible, if not to eat much, at least to breathe and to rest a little. Those who missed this break in the journey were at their worst.

A Soviet writer tells of one such party of men. Before they had had time to recover from their train journey they were marched a distance of several miles towards the port. There was a hitch over the supply of bread, so the men went off on empty stomachs. After an hour or two in the broiling sun they began to collapse; some of them died on the spot. The survivors sat down and declared that they would go no further until they were given bread. Such an organised protest was a rare occurrence among 'politicals', who had all been Party members and were used to discipline. The frightened guards went berserk, kicked the dead bodies about after the manner of the Good Soldier Schweik's doctors ('Take this malingerer to the morgue') and shot several stragglers who 'attempted to escape'.[4]

There were lesser inconveniences too. After hours of shunting on the way to the piers,

As the people I had under supervision were all sick, they asked me for permission to leave their place long enough to relieve themselves. Being 'protected' personnel I addressed myself in turn to a soldier watching us, and asked him to grant permission for the sick to do so. I did it in the official Russian form: 'Is it allowed by you that some sick people should attend to their urgent necessities?' 'Those who are bored with life,' the officer replied, 'should just make one step out of the column and they will be through with it!'[31]

And so, finally, the columns wound down to the boats. It was for the great majority of the prisoners their first sight of the open sea, for almost all of them their first sea voyage. On the Russians, in particular, the effect of the long cruise northward over the open ocean greatly enhanced the feeling already common to prisoners that they had been removed from the ordinary world. It seemed not merely a transportation from the 'mainland' (as the prisoners always referred to the rest of the country) merely to some distant penal island, but even to another 'planet', as Kolyma was always called in its songs and sayings.

One of the many more recent unofficial ballads about the camps (the widespread singing of which by Soviet students in private groups so strikingly illustrates the way in which Stalin's terror still haunts the Russian consciousness) is Galich's 'Magadan'.[3] It begins:

I remember Vanino port
Where the grim-looking steamer rode,
How we climbed the gangplank aboard
To the cold and gloomy hold. . . .

The ships of Kolyma's Middle Passage were mainly tramp steamers built at Flensburg and Newcastle, Schiedam and Tacoma, which had previously had such names as (ironically enough) *Commerical Quaker* or *Puget Sound*. They were mostly in the range of 5000 to 7000 gross tons, though some were as small as not much more than 2000 tons. The biggest, the *Nikolai Yezhov* (changed when he became an unperson to *Felix Dzerzhinsky*), was just over 9000 tons. She had originally been a cable ship, and it had caused considerable surprise when the Soviet government bought her in the mid-thirties, since it was not known to be conducting or planning any laying of cables. Such, however, was not the intention. The huge cable holds made splendid floating dungeons. However, there seem to have been disadvantages. At any rate many years later she was turned into a fisheries vessel. At the other end of the scale was the *Indigirka* , built at Greenock in 1886 and grossing only 2336 tons, which finally proved unable to ride the Okhotsk storms, and sank in December 1939.

The shipwreck of another prison vessel with the loss of 5000 prisoners and an escort of 200 is noted in July 1949. And there were other losses, such as the reported blowing up of the ship *Dalstroy* in Nakhodka harbour in 1946, apparently by Latvian and Lithuanian nationalists among the prisoners. The convicts had not yet gone aboard but supplies of ammonal, the explosive used in the gold mines, had already been loaded. Great destruction was caused in the town. There was no proof of responsibility, but many Latvians and Lithuanians seem to have been shot.

The core of the slave fleet were the *Dzhurma*, the *Dalstroy* and (from 1940) the *Sovlatvia*, which operated on the route throughout most of the period. The *Dzhurma*, of just under 7000 tons, was built in Holland in 1921. The *Dalstroy*, also of Dutch origin, had the same tonnage. The *Sovlatvia*, of just over 4000 tons, was built in Sweden for the independent Latvian government in 1926, and taken over after the Soviet annexation of that republic.

These ships were actually part of Dalstroy's (the NKVD Far Northern Construction Trust's) own fleet, as were for long periods vessels such as the *Felix Dzerzhinsky* and the *Kulu*; and their port of registry was Nagayevo itself. Each bore a broad white band with a blue stripe on its smokestack, and the letters DS for Dalstroy (the blue and white officially signifying hope). Other ships, registered in Vladivostok or Nakhodka, served mainland administrations and were made available for the Nagayevo run by arrangement.

Mrs Ginzburg describes the *Dzhurma* in 1939, when the ship had many years ahead of her on the Nagayevo run: 'She was an old ship that had seen better days. Her railings, stairways and even the captain's megaphone were dull and covered with verdigris. Now she was used solely for moving convicts.'[4]

She is first reported in these waters in 1933 when she sailed, laden with an above-capacity load of prisoners said to have numbered as many as 12,000, from Vladivostok through the Bering Straits to Ambarchik at the mouth of the Kolyma. Reaching the Arctic Ocean too late in the season, she was caught in the pack ice near Wrangel Island for the whole winter, arriving the following spring with no survivors among the prisoners.

Aboard the *Dzhurma* or another of the convict fleet, the prisoners were herded into the holds. Iron grilles cut these into isolated sections, and there were machine-gun nests on the decks. But the main recourse against riot or rebellion was the fire pumps, by which the icy ocean water could be and was directed at the prisoners.

The prisoners were kept under hatches (with brief and occasional exceptions) for the whole trip. One reason was that the ships went through the Straits of La Pérouse. They were thus, until 1945, running between Japanese territories, well in sight of land, and among Japanese shipping and fishing boats. At least one early (1932) case of a prisoner managing nevertheless to jump off and get picked up is recorded. But normally there was no trouble. The guards put on civilian clothes. The machine-guns disappeared from the bridge. The ships even had false papers made out in case of any incident.

A typical hold is described as having three decks, each containing two-level bunks made of poles.[32] The extent to which the prisoners were packed in, and the squalor, may be judged from Eugenia Ginzburg's remark that aboard the *Dzhurma*, 'How we longed for the comfort of Van 7'—the goods truck in which she had spent a month on the way to Vladivostok from Yaroslavl prison, 'so many pushed in that there scarcely seemed room to stand'; into which, though they could hardly stir, and could not even turn on their sides unless they all did it together, fifteen more women were pushed en route; in which 'it was so stuffy that the air felt thick and greasy . . .'; in which the roof of the wagon was red-hot and the nights were not long enough to cool it; in which the only ventilation was a three-inch gap closed while in stations; in which the water ration had been one mugful a day for all purposes; in which their inadequate bread ration had been cut to half as a penal measure . . . It was still better than the *Dzhurma*![4]

A male prisoner working in the sick bay of the *Sovlatvia* in 1949 tells of conditions aboard:

When we reached the women's hold, the entrance was

barred by two armed soldiers, but on seeing our red cross armbands, they let us pass. We climbed down a very steep, slippery wooden stairway with great difficulty and finally reached the bottom. It took us some time to accustom our eyes to the dim light of the dingy lower deck.

As I began to see where we were, my eyes beheld a scene which neither Goya nor Gustave Doré could ever have imagined. In that immense, cavernous, murky hold were crammed more than 2000 women. From the floor to the ceiling, as in a gigantic poultry farm, they were cooped up in open cages, five of them in each nine-foot-square space. The floor was covered with more women. Because of the heat and humidity, most of them were only scantily dressed; some had even stripped down to nothing. The lack of washing facilities and the relentless heat had covered their bodies with ugly red spots, boils, and blisters. The majority were suffering from some form of skin disease or other, apart from stomach ailments and dysentery.

At the bottom of the stairway we had just climbed down stood a giant cask, on the edges of which, in full view of the soldiers standing on guard above, women were perched like birds, and in the most incredible positions. There was no shame, no prudery, as they crouched there to urinate or to empty their bowels. One had the impression that they were some half-human, half-bird creatures which belonged to a different world and a different age. Yet seeing a man coming down the stairs, although a mere prisoner like themselves, many of them began to smile and some even tried to comb their hair. Who were these women? And where had they come from? I asked myself. I soon learned that they had been arrested all over Russia and those countries of Europe overrun by Soviet armies. The main accusation against them was collaboration with the enemy.[31]

Battened down in the murky holds there was nothing to see or do. Nothing, that is, except to survive the activities of the common criminals. Every report of these voyages tells of little else.

Though some of the prisoners had previously come across this great criminal element, the *urkas*, and been terrorised and robbed in camps, on trains or in the transit camp itself, for many the ships were the scene of their first encounter with this dreadful underground culture which had survived, with its own traditions and laws, since the Time of Troubles at the beginning of the seventeenth century, and had greatly increased in numbers by recruiting orphans and broken men of the revolutionary and collectivisation periods.

One woman tells us:

During the entire voyage, which lasted a week, no member of the guard on the ship's crew ever entered the prisoners' hold. They were afraid to, especially when a large number of murderers and bandits were being transported, since they were an insignificant, though heavily armed, minority compared to the number of prisoners. They stood with raised guns, ready to fire, when the prisoners were let out on deck in small groups to use the toilet. None of them took any account of what went on below decks. As a result, during all such voyages the criminals put across a reign of terror. If they want the clothing of any of the counter-revolutionaries, they take it from him. If the counter-revolutionary offers any resistance, he is beaten up. The old and weak are robbed of their bread. On every transport ship a number of prisoners die as a result of such treatment.[13]

General Gorbatov was robbed again:

While we were in the Sea of Okhotsk misfortune befell me. Early in the morning, when I was lying half-awake as many of us did, two 'trusties' came up to me and dragged away my boots which I was using as a pillow. One of them hit me hard on the chest and then on the head and said with a leer: 'Look at him—sells me his boots days ago, pockets the cash, and then refuses to hand them over!'

Off they went with their loot, laughing for all they were worth and only stopping to beat me up again when, out of sheer despair, I followed them and asked for the boots back. The other 'trusties' watched, roaring with laughter. 'Let him have it! Quit yelling—they're not your boots now.'

Only one of the political prisoners spoke up: 'Look, what are you up to? How can he manage in bare feet?' One of the thieves took off his pumps and threw them at me.

I had often heard, since I had been in prison, stories about the bestial behaviour of the common convicts but to be honest I never thought they would rob with such impunity in the presence of other prisoners. Anyhow, I lost my boots. Our guards, including their chief, got on well with the 'trusties', encouraged them to violence and used them to mock the 'enemies of the people'.[5]

Some of the most lurid accounts are of the women criminals. Eugenia Ginzburg recalls, in 1939:

But the worst was yet to come: our first meeting with the real hardened criminals among whom we were to live at Kolyma. When it seemed as though there were no room left for even a kitten, down through the hatchway poured another few hundred human beings. They were the cream of the criminal world: murderers, sadists, adepts at every kind of sexual perversion. To this day I remain convinced that the proper place for such people is a psychiatric hospital, not a prison or a camp. When I saw this half-naked, tattooed, ape-like horde invade the hold, I thought that it had been decided that we were to be killed off by mad women.

The fetid air reverberated to their shrieks, their ferocious obscenities, their wild laughter and their caterwaulings. They capered about, incessantly stamping their feet even though there appeared to be no room to put a foot down. Without wasting any time they set about terrorising and bullying the 'ladies'—the politicals—delighted to find that the 'enemies of the people' were creatures even more despised and outcast than themselves. Within five minutes we had a thorough introduction to the law of the jungle. They seized our bits of bread, snatched the last of our rags out of our bundles, pushed us out of the places we had managed to find. Some of us wept, some panicked, some tried to reason with the whores, some spoke very politely to them hoping to restore their self-respect. Others called for the warders; they might have saved their breath, for throughout the whole voyage we never saw a single representative of authority other than the sailor who brought a cartload of bread to the mouth of the hold and threw our 'rations' down to us as though we were a cageful of wild beasts.[4]

A half-blind Polish woman, in 1944, tells:

One hundred and thirty women were also taken, of whom I was one. In all there were taken five of us Polish women, a few Soviet politicals, and all the rest of that type of criminal which can be most nearly described by the European expression apache.

When at last we went aboard it was dark and I was quite blind. Heavy rain began to fall. Nobody helped me. I was in danger of being left completely alone on the desolate shore. Another blind woman (Soviet) at last came to my aid and finally a soldier. The idea that I might have been left behind amused everybody immensely. In the darkness hands reached out towards me from all sides. One tore off the shawl, the Polish shawl I wore on my head. Others tried to drag off my sweater and seize my sack. We fought in the darkness of the night and of my blindness. I hit out at random; wherever there seemed to be anything soft. I could just make out the lamp swinging; I could taste blood, and I knew that somehow I must get my back against a wall. I meant to fight to the last. If I once gave in I knew they would murder me. As I reached out and a blow went wide I fell against a door opening, and the commandant appeared. For the time being I was saved.

All the way to Kolyma my battle with the apache women went on. One befriended me for a while and then herself completely robbed me. She simply could not keep it up. Her name was Lola and she looked like the old female wolf who leads the pack. Somewhere she had some Polish blood too.

For the few days that she was my friend she shared her bread with me.

The retching, the wild cries, the dancing and stamping of feet, the brawling, fornicating and wild-cat fighting went on night and day. Even the men were afraid of these women. The commandant was afraid of them too. Nevertheless, he helped me to get some things back. I said to one woman, 'You are so young, you are even beautiful, and yet you are as evil as the fiend himself. Why?' She looked at me with an expression of which I can give no idea. 'Why should I be otherwise? Hell is where I live and the fiend is my brother.'[2]

Elinor Lipper describes a particular danger that threatened the political women, from the men criminals:

We lay squeezed together on the tarred floor of the hold because the criminals had taken possession of the plank platform. If one of us dared to raise her head, she was greeted by a rain of fishheads and entrails from above. When any of the seasick criminals threw up, the vomit came down upon us. At night, the men criminals bribed the guard, who was posted on the stairs to the hold, to send over a few women for them. They paid the guard in bread that they had stolen from their fellow prisoners.[13]

Not only criminals worked this trade, indeed:

Some of the girls had better luck and were entertained by the captain, the chief mate, the battalion commander, and other officers who treated themselves to the charms of these unfortunate women on their way to the wastes of Kolyma. Girls were invited to cabins where they were offered a decent meal, good liquor, and the luxury of a shower, clean towel, and clean bed sheets. They realised, of course, that this might be the last chance they would have for such luxuries.[31]

But sex was not always so peaceable a transaction:

In 1944 several hundred young girls came to Kolyma. They were the so-called *ukazniki*, sent out here for unauthorised absences from a war factory, or for some similar minor offence. . . . The criminals, who formed the greater part of the human freight aboard this ship, had an absolutely free hand in the hold. They broke through the wall into the room where the female prisoners were kept and raped all the women who took their fancy. A few male prisoners who tried to protect the women were stabbed to death. Several old men had their bread snatched from them day after day, and died of starvation. One of the criminals, who appropriated a woman whom the leader of the band had marked for his own, had his eyes put out with a needle.[13]

This, in accord with their own 'Law'. Another prisoner, a Polish woman, reports a similar sanction aboard another ship: 'From the men's quarters came cries which surpassed any I had heard before. The apache men settling a score with their knives. A brigade leader had gambled and lost the brigade's bread ration at cards. For this he had been tried by the men apaches and found guilty. They literally cut him up with their knives. His brains lay scattered on the decks.'[2]

As to the needle-wielding gang, 'When the ship arrived in Magadan and the prisoners were driven out of the hold, fifteen were missing; they had been murdered by the criminals during the voyage and the guards had not lifted a finger. The upshot of this particularly glaring scandal was that after the facts became known in Magadan, the commander of the ship's guard was called on the carpet and arrested.'[13]

On another occasion, in 1949, a bunch of ruffians had pushed through the rust-weakened bulkhead into the women's hold, and had tried to rape them. Soldiers had intervened and some of the rampaging prisoners had been killed. 'As we filed towards the ship's gangway I observed a few prisoners in chains. They were the ringleaders of the assault on the women's quarters who had not been shot.

Two of them, teenagers, were charged with having hanged a woman who tried to resist their attack. Both looked quite calm and asked for a smoke.'[31]

An incident which is described as taking place on the *Dzhurma* in the latter half of 1939 is given by three prisoners, two Soviet and one Western, none of whom was present, but who learnt of it from witnesses. The accounts are slightly different, but the value of authentication through such evidently independent corroboration is obvious: we shall come across it again.

Mrs Lipper says: 'The criminals succeeded in breaking through the wall of the hold and getting at the provisions. They robbed the stores and then, to wipe out the traces, set the storeroom on fire. There was a frightful panic among the prisoners who were locked in the hold of the burning ship. The fire was held in check, but the *Dzhurma* entered port still burning.'[13]

As Mrs Ginzburg describes it, '—a fire broke out. The male criminals seized the opportunity to try to break out and were battened down into a corner of the hold. When they went on rioting, the crew hosed them down to keep them quiet. Then they forgot about them. As the fire was still burning the water boiled and the wretched men died in it. For a long time afterwards the *Dzhurma* stank intolerably.'[4] The third account, from a woman Social-Revolutionary, is similar.[22]

This may well also be the same occasion as one given as happening the previous year in *The Gulag Archipelago*:

The thieves aboard got out of the hold and into the storage room, plundered it, and set it afire. The ship was very close to Japan when this occurred. Smoke was pouring from it, and the Japanese offered help, but the captain refused to accept it and *even refused to open the hatches*. When Japan had been left behind, the corpses of those suffocated by smoke were thrown overboard and the half-burned, half-spoiled food aboard was sent on to camp as rations for the prisoners.[32]

A particularly unpleasant trip. There were other arrivals at Nagayevo harbour in specially nasty circumstances, as when a convoy of four ships on the first voyage of the season in 1938 was unable to penetrate the late-lasting ice, and disembarked the prisoners so that they had to finish the voyage on foot over the ice-pack, 'tormented half-dead people in that grey line . . . carrying on their shoulders other half-dead people—sufferers from arthritis or prisoners without legs'.[32]

Or again, on 5 December 1947 the steamer *Kim* arrived with the last cargo of the year. On it were 3000 prisoners who had been drenched with fire hoses during the trip, in the course of putting down some sort of riot. The temperature was −40°C. There were many dead, who were carried by lorries to the common grave without post-mortem or certificate; and many more needed amputations or other treatment.

But even the normal arrival at that coast is always described as a moment of gloom. Even in August, a sea the colour of lead washed a rockbound shore, under cliffs up to a thousand feet high. Nagayevo, though a splendid external harbour, is outstanding for its harshness even on the notoriously inhospitable shores of the Sea of Okhotsk, and for nearly three hundred years of Russian settlement it had been left deserted.

The prisoners disembarked. The dead and the very sick were laid out on the stony beach and checked. The remainder were formed up for the march to the Magadan transit camp, a few miles away from the coast.

They found themselves in a strange land.

CHAPTER TWO

INTO KOLYMA

THE Kolyma Region consists, mainly, of the basin of the Kolyma River, which winds northward from its source in the Gydan or Kolyma Range till it reaches the East Siberian Sea near Ambarchik: a vast area about the size of the Ukraine. To this has been annexed a strip of coastal territory to the south of the watershed, including Magadan, the capital. The climate of this southern strip, where the prisoners arrive, is less extreme than most of the river basin, though cold enough by most standards. The sea, for example, is frozen for scores of miles out from shore for five months of the year. Nevertheless the mildness of Magadan, Nagayevo and their surroundings, where the temperature has never fallen below −50°C., is often remarked on by prisoners coming from northerly areas.

General Gorbatov says, 'When I had first reached Magadan from Vladivostok it had seemed a wild place to me. Now, after Maldyak, Magadan seemed cosy and the air quite different, as if I had gone in November from the north of Russia to Sochi on the Black Sea Coast.'[5]

The climate of the interior, where it may go down to − 70°C., is indeed the coldest in the Northern Hemisphere: the actual Pole of Cold is at Oymyakon, just over the Gydan.

A camp rhyme ran:

> Kolyma, Kolyma
> Chudnaya planeta
> Dvenadsat mesyatsov zima
> Ostalnoye leto.

> (Kolyma, Kolyma
> Wonderful planet:
> Twelve months winter,
> The rest summer.)

This is an exaggeration. The brief Arctic summer melts the snow, and the soil, to a depth of about six feet. In fact the hundred days of the mining season proper take place when the topsoil is at least warm enough to melt fairly easily when a fire is built on it, together with the two-month period when it is actually melted. At the same time the rivers unfreeze.

But the Kolyma summer is almost as treacherous as the winter. The ground becomes warm, especially on the southern slopes. But in some areas the swamps may go no deeper than a few feet, so that a road worker would be standing in ice while being baked.

In addition, the insects are truly abominable, in particular in the coastal region. One specially large type of gadfly can sting through deer hide, and drives horses crazy. The local tribesmen, however accustomed to the insects, always dress heavily and wear mittens and netting over their heads—clothing which was not issued to prisoners after the first years.

The freezing swamps of the upper valleys of the Kolyma basin were variegated by small hills, or *sopki*, on which settlements were often built.

The main gold deposits are in and around the upper reaches of the Kolyma and its tributaries: that is to say, in the more southerly section of the river basin, though the history of the area since 1932 is one of the continual discovery and exploitation of new deposits.

The area had been roughly known to the Russians for centuries. The first effective Russian crossing of the Urals came in the 1580s, when Yermak led his famous expedition. But within an incredibly short span they had reached the Pacific. The Kolyma basin itself had been explored by 1650—Nizhne-Kolymsk, near the mouth of the river, had been founded as a trading post as early as 1644.

In fact, paradoxical though it may seem, the far north of Siberia was penetrated and exploited before the more southerly areas. In those days, the north was swarming with every type of fur-producing animal, and in particular the unrivalled sable. Just as the Hudson Bay Company, in parallel circumstances, held a fur-trading empire in the far north of western Canada as early as the late eighteenth century, so in Siberia it was to the arctic and sub-arctic lands that the adventurer or merchant was first attracted.

The area was held by a handful of widely-scattered settlements or forts, between which bands of hunters sought out their prey. From 1700, silver and tin mines were operating elsewhere in Siberia, and in 1745 at Nerchinsk, near the Mongolian border, some gold was obtained as a by-product. Early in the nineteenth century gold deposits proper were discovered at Nerchinsk and later in the Yenisey and Lena valleys. It was at first a state monopoly but private prospecting was allowed in 1826 and ten years later private operation of gold finds was also allowed, though the gold had to be delivered to the state.

With the comparative exhaustion of the furs, gold became an important Siberian resource, but it was still on nothing like the scale that eventually developed in the Kolyma basin.

The first gold in Kolyma seems to have been found in 1910 when a fugitive convict sold some to a trader. His name, or diminutive, survives—Boriska—and the first gold mine was called Boriskin. However, nothing was done until in 1925 a White officer called Nikolayev, who had been hiding out since the end of the anti-Bolshevik operations in 1922, took advantage of the 1925 amnesty and brought in some platinum. Prospecting parties were now sent into Kolyma. By the end of the twenties private traders were bringing interesting quantities down a track over the Gydan to the mouth of the Ola River. It was becoming clear that the Kolyma fields were exceptional, something like the equivalent of a Soviet Alaska. ˜

Mining began in 1927, at first with free labour, though less than 200 men were involved. The government permitted them free enterprise and only maintained the old monopoly of gold purchasing. In this it was outbidden by legal or semi-legal private traders. These were the first to cut a direct route through the taiga to the Sea of Okhotsk.

The government was faced with great difficulty. On the face of it, it could either give concessions to free enterprise or invest a great amount of capital in the development of the area. But the first was ruled out for political reasons and there was no capital available. The solution was to make use of the one reserve material the government could dispose of—human beings. By 1930, when the position became clear, the first great forced-labour projects were starting, manned by 'kulaks'. In December 1931 Dalstroy, the Far Northern Construction Trust, was set up, in charge of all forced-labour projects in the north-east of Siberia. Reingold Berzin, a Latvian Communist, was appointed its head.

Dalstroy seems at first to have covered the new Kolyma region only. Eventually gold was also found on the Indigirka to the west, and this and various other areas of development such as the Chukhotsk peninsula gradually came under Dalstroy control. At the height of its operations,

Dalstroy, which was an NKVD agency, coming directly under the Police Ministry in Moscow, controlled an enormous area, though its headquarters remained at Magadan. This area has never been precisely defined but it seems to have included all the territory beyond the Lena north of the Aldan as far as the Bering Straits: a territory four times the size of France. (And if it is true that in 1953 Dalstroy's then chief, Derevenko, was held responsible for the labour camp rebellion at Norilsk, it must then have stretched as far west as the Yenisey and controlled a region as large as non-Soviet Europe.)

In all this vast area, the normal Soviet administration did not operate, and Dalstroy itself was in charge of all the activities of government. Thus, in Dalstroy's early days its Head simultaneously controlled the Kolyma camps. As its operations spread, its Head had a deputy responsible specifically for the Kolyma camps, whose post was Head of USVITL (the Administration of the North-Eastern Corrective Labour Camps).

After Berzin fell in 1937, if we may anticipate, he was replaced as Head of Dalstroy by Pavlov, while the ill-famed Major Garanin became Head of USVITL and responsible for the Kolyma operations proper. Garanin was shot in 1939. His successors fell rapidly, Vyshnevetsky coming to grief with a disastrous first attempt to open up the Pestraya Dresva area in 1940.

Meanwhile Pavlov had fallen, apparently owing to a quarrel with Beria about production plans, and he was replaced by the dreadful Ivan Nikishov, who seems to have held the post until the end of the war. His successor, Major-General Derevenko, lasted until 1953, about the end of the era.

Known successive heads of the two organisations are, with appropriate dates:

Dalstroy	USVITL
E. P. Berzin 1932-7	I. G. Filipov 1937
K. A. Pavlov 1937-40	Maj. Garanin 1938-9
I. F. Nikishov 1940-6	Maj. Yegorov 1939-40
P. P. Derevenko 1946-53	Col. Vyshnevetsky 1940
	Col. Gakayev 1941
	Col. Drabkin 1942-

In 1931-2, the decision was taken to base the campaign to exploit Kolyma on the splendid harbour of Nagayevo, several miles long and well protected from the wind by its high cliffs, in spite of its other disadvantages. It was impossible to build a real settlement at Nagayevo, so the operational base was set up beyond the cliffs some miles inland in a swampy area on the edge of the polar taiga. Here, in the early thirties, the settlement of Magadan was begun.

In the summer of 1932, the operation was launched. The collectivisation assault on the peasantry had produced a vast expansion in the number of arrests. Of the 10 million 'kulaks' disposed of, half probably died in famine and by execution, and of the remainder certainly no fewer than $3\frac{1}{2}$ million poured into the prison camps. Kolyma got its share.

Throughout the navigational season scores of thousands of prisoners were put ashore at Nagayevo. It was a typical operation of the time, in that it was insufficiently prepared, the conditions had not been adequately investigated, and the programme was impossibly ambitious. This had to be made up for by simple human-wave tactics.

Though the prisoners were treated ruthlessly, it was not with the mean and vicious ruthlessness of later years. They were not deprived of food and clothing simply to procure their destruction. It was rather that, since everything else took priority over the prisoners' well-being, they were (for example) made to live in tents while hewing and placing the pier stones, cutting roads through the rocks, and beginning to set up the buildings of Magadan.

This was, of course, the period in which the Soviet Union was engaged in the struggle for collectivisation and industrialisation, and famine ravaged the rural areas. Supplies were naturally short for everybody, and prisoners were the first to suffer. The ration at this time was two pounds of bread; hot soup in the morning; fatless gruel at noon; hot water at night.

The winter of 1932–3 was exceptionally severe, with blinding snowstorms. It was impossible at times even to walk from one house to another in the middle of Magadan itself. The camps set up in the taiga were often completely cut off. Supplies failed, and in some camps, when communications were restored, it was found that no one was left, not even the dogs. According to one story a convoy lost its way in the Shaidinsky valley and died, several thousand prisoners with their guards, to a man. Survivors of the first year said that only one out of 50 or 100 of those 'thrown' into the first mass assault on the Kolyma gold came back.

One prisoner records:

In March 1933, 600 prisoners were sent to Gold Mine No. 1 of the Mining Administration of the North . . . there were two other administrations of the same kind, those of the West and the South. We set off on foot on this long journey. We had to travel 370 miles in deep snow and during terribly cold weather to the Khatenakh *sopka*.

We had to make 16 miles a day, after which we spent the night in tents set up on the snow. After our scanty rations in the morning, we set out again. Those who were unable to survive this long gruelling march and died on the way were left with the snow for their only tomb. Our guards forbade us to give them a proper burial. Those who lagged behind were shot by the guards, without stopping the column. For thirty long days we trudged along over the immense expanses of snow, arriving at last exhausted at the *sopka* of

Khatenakh, where we were quartered in tents already awaiting us.[10]

When the navigation season opened again in 1933 the new prisoners were sent up along the winter route, to build the highway to Srednikan and thence to Seimchan, where the Kolyma becomes navigable. This had the usual difficulties of road construction in a land of rivers and mountains. But in addition the thaw which now melted the upper levels of the permafrost made the whole ground intractably difficult. One section of the highway hardly a mile long is said to have swallowed over 80,000 beams and even years later was far from being firmly established, requiring repairs every year. These problems had not been properly allowed for. And, moreover, the route chosen from a too sketchy survey proved impractical, and a considerably longer one had to be followed. As a result the road was two years behind schedule, and was only properly finished in 1937.

The heavy work on the roads and in the newly opened mining areas took its toll among the exhausted prisoners. The summer of 1933 is said to have cost more in human lives than even the previous winter.

In 1934, the situation improved somewhat, and in 1935 Berzin was able to start the exploitation of Kolyma on a rational basis. And now, for a couple of years—until late 1937—Kolyma went through what Shalamov calls its 'golden age'.

All prisoners' accounts agree that Berzin instituted a system by which the labour of the prisoners was efficiently and (as far as conditions permitted) humanely used. It is said that he sought and obtained special permission from Stalin for this exceptionally careful handling of human resources to the maximum advantage. For he saw that a prisoner who was warm, well-fed and not overworked was likely to be more productive. And Stalin, at the time, needed gold from Kolyma more than he needed its punitive capacity. Under this regime gold production naturally soared.

We have spoken of the harshness of the Kolyma climate. But it is not unhealthy to men kept well fed and properly clothed. One prisoner sent there in 1935 who had become tubercular in jail and transit camp says that his tuberculosis was actually cured by the climate, and that a doctor at Vladivostok had predicted this.

Shalamov tells us of 'Excellent nourishment, good clothing, 4 to 6 hours work in winter, 10 hours in summer'. Lipper speaks of the food as 'adequate when arrival of supplies was not hampered by transportation difficulties—and prisoners who worked well were entitled to additional food bought at the camp commissary'. Vodka was even provided in the ration, during the cold weather, as both Lipper and Petrov tell us. Even more important, Lipper confirms that 'in winter the prisoners were given fur coats, fur caps and warm felt boots'.

At the same time, 'the prisoners received good pay' (Shalamov); 'the prisoners. . . . were well paid' (Petrov). They were able to send money to their families.

Berzin even provided a non-material incentive. Shalamov tells us that 'The count of labour-days was managed in such a way that prisoners condemned for ten years were let out after two or three.' At this point, indeed, this Soviet witness who (like Lipper but unlike Petrov) was not there before 1937, oversimplifies the degree of 'liberalization' possible even in the most liberal of Stalinist periods and places. Lipper has to qualify all her comments with the remark that in general, 'Even in those days, however, the treatment of criminals was considerably better than that of counter-revolutionaries. And for the most part only criminals were given time off their sentences for satisfactory work, which was a great incentive to their working well.'[13]

Petrov is more specific:

In those days in the Kolyma there was also a very high credit for working days—a shortening of the sentence for those who worked. Men sentenced for criminal acts received credit for 100–150 days per year, and sometimes for 200. Those sentenced for counter-revolution only on 58–10 (agitation) received 50 days credit per year. Only the remaining others who had been sentenced on the more serious articles of the code received no credit at all.[23]

Even so, the better physical treatment went with, and implied, a fairly humane psychological relationship with the prisoners. And this in turn meant that the criminal element was not at this time used by the administration as an instrument for terrorising the politicals, but was held in reasonable check.

It is also true that in this earlier period the prisoners had not experienced conditions in jail and in transit as crowded, as ill-fed and as unhealthy as became normal under Yezhov. And these earlier prisoners had a much lower proportion of intellectuals and a higher one of peasants, not only stronger and more adjusted to and experienced in outdoor physical labour, but also less amenable to bullying by urkas.

In retrospect, then, the period was idyllic. The frightful casualties of the first years were almost forgotten. The fact that the political prisoners should not have been there at all, being innocent of anything except a critical attitude to Stalin—and more often not even that—was not the fault of the local authorities. And elsewhere in Russia things were already far worse.

But the end of the Berzin era was approaching. At the June 1937 Plenum of the Central Committee, Stalin personally attacked the practice which, he said, had come into force, of 'coddling' prisoners. Throughout the USSR the response was a vast increase in brutality. A decision to extend this to Kolyma came shortly. NKVD chief Yezhov, certainly with Stalin's approval, specifically denounced conditions in the area 'with indignation' at a meeting of the Central Committee—evidently the one held on 11–12 October 1937.

The fall of Berzin and his associates naturally followed. Berzin had been put up as a candidate in the election then being held for the Supreme Soviet, but a week before the voting prisoners noted that his portraits disappeared and his name was withdrawn.

There seems to have been some apprehension that, on the basis of his powerful and quasi-independent fief, Berzin might offer resistance. An NKVD delegation arrived with promises of awards and promotion, feted him in Magadan, and only arrested him on the airfield, of which their members had by then taken control. He was taken to Moscow, to be shot, apparently as a Japanese spy, on 11 November 1939. His wife was also jailed, as was then customary. The last ship of the season (as it happened the *Nikolai Yezhov*) meanwhile brought in hundreds of replacements for the lesser posts held by the Berzin gang. His close collaborators underwent the same fate; his deputy Filipov died or committed suicide in Magadan prison, Alexei Yezorov, called 'Red Liochka', head of the Southern Administration, Tsyrko, head of the Northern Administration, Mayzuradze, Vaskov . . .

But the Berzin affair also involved (as Shalamov tells us) 'the arrest and execution of several thousand people and the infliction of severe penalties on several thousand others, prisoners or otherwise: commandants of mines, of camps, of sectors; instructors; secretaries of Party committees; heads of gangs; senior prisoners; brigade leaders. . .'.[28]

At first this wave of arrests, though causing apprehension, did not appear to the ordinary prisoners to signify any basic change. In the Northern Administration a prisoner noted the arrest of its Chief Engineer, Eidlin, of the Heads and Chief Engineers of a number of mines and of many other free employees—and the renaming of the Berzin mine as 'At-Urakh'. He and his mates were aware of 'endless secret conferences of Party members' with the new Head of the Region's Political Section. They saw barbed wire being set up everywhere, searchlights, machine-gun posts.

More definite rumours began to percolate: 'A friend who worked in the Planning Section . . . told me that Moscow revoked the earlier plan for gold production and sent in a new and much higher one. Our Administration was to receive an additional 30,000 prisoners . . .' And then:

Late at night, while Khudiakov, Stepanov and I were asleep in our room near the carpentry shop, someone knocked violently on the door. I opened it. Sukhanov entered, looking very upset.

'What has happened?' I asked.

'Be prepared for very unpleasant things. There has just been a meeting of the leading personnel of the Administration. We were informed of new instructions from Pavlov, the chief of Dalstroy. We are ordered to remove immediately from administrative posts all prisoners sentenced for counter-revolution and send them to general work at the mines. All the other prisoners can remain temporarily only at the most common, non-responsible work.'[23]

This was the first blow in the mass terror against the prisoners which now ensued. The year that followed was the most frightful the camps had known. Previous years had seen, on occasion, massive casualties. But these had been due to inefficiencies in supply, attempts to carry out assignments in impossible conditions, and in fact—if in exaggerated form—the normal incompetence and brutality of Soviet life. When the difficulties could be overcome, conditions, as we have seen, were tolerable. But above all, prisoners were not subjected to lethal conditions on purpose.

Now came a regime under which the prisoners' chances of survival, even if they escaped the wave of executions which ensued, were reduced to a minimum. Not only was the ration system made so inadequate that survival, except by the holders of 'functions', such as clerk or nurse, became impossible over any long period, but even such disgusting harassments took place as the banning of adequate clothing. Under newly enforced regulations, fur clothing was banned and replaced by wadding jackets and trousers 'which soon hung like torn rags upon the bodies of the gaunt prisoners'.[13] Felt boots were similarly replaced by canvas shoes. The result, the only result, was, as was clearly intended, a great increase in suffering and in death. This single point illustrates more clearly than anything else the animus of the new authorities.

Everywhere those in charge of the camps were given higher and higher production targets. At the same time their human raw material became increasingly weaker and less effective. Those who arrived from the 'mainland', mostly townsmen, had experienced the intensely debilitating effects of the Yezhov prison regime and of the cattle trucks and rations and of Vladivostok transit camp. In Kolyma they were driven directly to hard physical labour for which they were quite unfitted. The newly introduced ration scales were barely sufficient even for those who fulfilled their full norms and impossible for others. As output dropped the local NKVD commandants had no option but to increase working hours so that a vicious circle was established. The only way the system could be kept going at all was that as the 'goners' died out, they were replaced by a continual stream of new prisoners. One estimate is that henceforward every kilogram of gold cost one human life.

CHAPTER THREE

1938—BAPTISM OF HORROR

AND so Kolyma entered its long period as the worst and deadliest of all the labour camp areas. There were 'good' years and bad years in the epoch which followed. None was to be quite as bad as 1938 itself; but none was to be more than a comparative relief. Meanwhile, as the winter of 1937–8 set in, the 'tempest', as prisoners described it, began to rage more and more violently.

The first major policy decision was to insist on winter work in the mines though, as Petrov points out, this was highly uneconomic—especially as regards labour. The prisoners did find that 'work in the mine held one vast advantage—it was relatively warm. There was no snow, no icy piercing wind. The steam which thawed out the sand also lent some warmth to the air. The water in the draining ditches froze only at the very exit of the mine.'

But there were also disadvantages. The boots were always wet, never quite drying out—rheumatism was guaranteed. Then, the air in the pit, where there was no ventilation whatsoever, was filled twice daily with the poisonous fumes of blasted ammonal. Only thirty minutes were allowed for the clearing of the fumes through the entrance of the mine, after which the workers were driven back into the pits to continue their work. Many of them succumbed to the poisoned atmosphere and coughed violently, spitting blood and often particles of lung. After a short time, these were usually sent either to the weak squads for lumbering, or to their graves. Mortality was especially high among the men who carted the wet sand from the barrack after the washing. From the steamy, damp atmosphere of the heater the perspiring wheelbarrow-pushers slipped through the opening, which was covered by an old blanket, rolling out their wheelbarrows into the piercing 50°-below-zero frost. The time limit in this work was, at the most, one month, after which either pneumonia or meningitis dispatched the worker into the next world.[23]

The new prisoners, moreover, were mainly people who had never done any physical work: 'Scientists, artists, politicians, educators, leaders of industry, trade, and government.'[13] A veteran prisoner describes them:

Their faces all showed signs of frostbite, although the winter was only three months old and the most severe frosts were yet to come. The majority of them were so dirty looking I was willing to wager that some of them had not washed their faces for weeks. Their clothes were like nothing I had ever seen at the Kolyma—everything from the torn boots to the incredibly dirty rags wrapped around their necks instead of scarves, their burned and tattered winter coats.

The men had starved, worn-out faces, quiet voices, were completely absorbed in themselves and uncommunicative. Their range of interest was limited to work and food, and more food, and food again. Besides work and food the other questions discussed among them were tobacco—the eternal Kolyma shag—and the cold.

They came to the tent after having supper in the dining room. They had rushed there as soon as they had returned to the camp from work—and immediately crowded around the stoves, coming so close that one feared they would catch fire. Indeed, now and again one heard voices: 'Look out! Your coat's burning!' The repulsive smell of burning rags would come up and bite into your nostrils.

The sight of these creatures who had almost lost the image of man made me feel distinctly uncomfortable. The possibility of becoming one of them seemed anything but attractive.[23]

Conditions killed them off quickly. But 'conditions' were assisted by a massive employment of execution as a reprisal against failure to produce adequate gold, and, in effect, on any pretext whatever.

The visible villain was Major, later Colonel, Garanin, the new Head of USVITL. His rule gave his name to a whole epoch of terror—the *Garaninshchina*, as with the *Yezhovshchina* which was sweeping the USSR as a whole.

Wholesale arrests began in the camp. As a rule the charge was systematic underfulfilment of quotas. Since no man in the gold field could possibly fulfil them, the failure was ascribed as criminal when the worker completed less than 50 per cent of the quota.

It was absolutely impossible to measure accurately the exact performance of a worker, and the estimate made depended entirely upon the attitude of the foremen. The foremen made daily measurements in a rough and ready fashion with the help of a tape line, and made their reports to the office where the volume of excavated sand was translated into percentages of the daily quota fulfilled by each brigade. In doing this a practice was systematically resorted to whereby a certain amount of work performed by the less efficient brigades was stolen from them and credited to the better brigades as a means of encouraging them. But the foremen were not altogether free in recording their measurements. Once a month a measurement of the mine's entire output was made by surveyors with instruments of great accuracy. The engineers measured the depth the mine increased during the month, and compared this with the added-up measurements of the foremen. When the figures disagreed—and they always did, and to a great extent—the foremen were merely reprimanded. Now, by Pavlov's new order, foremen guilty of excessive measurements were to be put on trial. The same order stated the fact that six foremen had been executed for deceiving the State. It was natural that the foremen often went to the other extreme—charity begins at home—and deliberately gave lower figures.

The official figures for labour productivity immediately dropped heavily.

Then the firing squad set to work.

A representative of the NKVD three-man court—the Troika— appeared at the gold field. He held conferences with the section heads and demanded lists from them of malicious saboteurs who systematically failed to make their quotas. The section heads had no alternative but to prepare such lists and to include in them the least able workers who lowered the average labour productivity for that section.[23]

Another veteran convict recalls:

In our mine the Third Section . . . was particularly active during the 1937–8 period. Some nights when we came back from work, the guards read out thirty to fifty names. The persons called had to step out of the ranks and were marched off immediately to the prison. The next morning they were driven in trucks to the Khatenakh *sopka*, where they were shot.

In the evening, in addition to the list of new victims, the guards would read us the announcement: 'By judgement of the camp command'—(then would follow the names of those who had been executed)—'shot for sabotage, ill-will, and agitation against the Soviet power.'[10]

—or, as Solzhenitsyn categorises the crimes (the announcement of which was followed by the pinning of the lists to the camp notice boards): 'for counter-revolutionary agitation', 'for insulting the guard', 'for failure to fulfil the work norm'.

Shalamov well develops what these offences amounted to:

'For counter-revolutionary agitation'. This was the way one of the paragraphs in Garanin's sentences began. For the man in the street in 1937 it hardly needed explaining what counter-revolutionary agitation was: Praising a Russian novel published abroad—ten years; declaring that one queued too long to buy soap—five years. . . . But in the camps there was none of this gradation: five, ten, twenty years. Say aloud that the work was harsh, mutter the most innocent remark about Stalin, keep silent while the crowd of prisoners yelled 'Long live Stalin', and you're shot—silence is agitation! . . . No trial, no investigation. The proceedings of the Troika, that famous institution, always meant death.

They shot also for 'outrage against a member of the guard'. Any insult, any insufficiently respectful reply, any 'discussion' when hit, or beaten up, any too disrespectful a gesture by a prisoner towards a guard was called 'an attempt at violence against the guard'.

They shot for 'refusal to work'. Thousands of prisoners died before understanding the mortal danger of their attitude. Old men at the end of their strength, exhausted and famished skeletons, incapable of walking a step to reach the camp gate in the morning when the columns wound towards the mine, stayed on their mattresses. They wrote their refusal on forms roneoed in advance: 'Although shod and clothed in conformity with the exigencies of the season . . .' The richer mines ran to properly printed forms where it was enough to write the name and a few points: 'date of birth, article of the law, duration of sentence'. Three refusals meant the execution platoon—'according to the law'. . . .

Even at the end of one's strength, one had to go to the mine; the gang chief signed every morning for this 'unit of production' and the administration counter-signed. This done the prisoner was saved, for this day he escaped death. Once out he could not work since he was incapable of it. He had to endure his day of torture to the end, but he was not classed as refractory. The administration could not then shoot the sick man; it hadn't, they said, 'the right'. I will not judge the extent of these rights, but for long years I struggled against myself to not refuse to go to the mine and to drag myself to the gates of the 'zone'.

The last heading—the richest—under which they shot prisoners by waves was 'non-fulfilment of norms'. This crime took entire brigades to the common graves. The authorities provided a theoretical basis for this rigour: all over the country the Five Year Plan was broken down into precise figures in each factory for each establishment. At Kolyma they were broken down for each gang. 'The Five Year Plan is the law! Not to carry out the Plan is a crime!'[28]

And so, in a camp, 'For more than a month, day and night, at each morning and evening roll call, an officer would read out the flowing lists of the condemned to death. At $-50°$C., musicians chosen from the common criminals would sound a fanfare before and after the reading of each document. . . . Each list invariably ended with the words: "The judgement has been executed. Chief of USVITL, Colonel Garanin."'[28]

According to various accounts, accepted by Roy Medvedev and others, Garanin himself used to walk down the line of prisoners on parade, shooting them when he felt like it: two soldiers followed him taking turns at loading his revolver. Perhaps, on occasion. But, according at least to Shalamov, who saw him some fifteen times on his visits to camps of the Northern Administration, this particular story is a legend: as 'chairman of the liquidation Troika', he was 'content to sign the decrees'. If Garanin personally did not shoot prisoners, at least in public, the story nevertheless seems to have a foundation in fact, as with lesser officials such as Nikolai Aglamov, Head of the Southern Camp Administration, who 'liked to select a brigade which was guilty of something from those paraded before him. He would order it to be led to one side—and himself shot the terrified people with his pistol as they huddled together, accompanying the operation with merry cries. The bodies were not buried; when May came they decomposed and then prisoners who had survived were summoned to bury them in return for increased rations and even alcohol.'[32]

This attitude to human life became common among the NKVD as a whole. A typical account is of a drunken NKVD officer appearing at a work site, accusing prisoners of stealing drinking bowls from the State (it was then quite common for them to carry their gruel to the work site to eat it) and shooting wildly at the group, killing one and wounding two others.[23]

In the women's camps, too, random killing was the norm. That year, 1 May and 7 November were celebrated by sending batches of prisoners, without other pretext, to the penalty cells, where many died. Then, on the usual parades, the order would be given for every tenth woman to be taken out and shot.[22] On one occasion thirty Polish women were shot in a batch at the Elgen camp.[32] Meanwhile starvation and epidemics took their toll, as in the men's camps.

Many camps became famous for their executions and mass graves: Orotukan, Polyarny Spring, Svistoplyas, Annushka and even the agricultural camp Dukcha.'[32] The Zolotisti mine had a particularly murderous reputation. There, Solzhenitsyn tells us, brigades 'were taken from the face during the day and shot one after the other on the spot. (This was not instead of executions at night—those went on as usual.)'[32]

On his formal rounds Garanin

took special note of those who were convicted of KRTD (counter-revolutionary Trotskyist activity).

'Which of these have not met their quota?' he would ask.

Most had not, could not. At evening roll call, when they returned from the mines, he would call out these unfortunates, revile them as saboteurs who were trying to continue their criminal counter-revolutionary Trotskyist activities even in camp, and he would have them driven in a herd out of the gate. At a short distance from the camp they would be shot *en masse* under his personal supervision.

This was still not enough. At night he would have thousands of enemies of the people taken out of all the Kolyma camps, loaded on to trucks and driven off to a prison. This prison, called Serpantinka, is about 375 miles west of Magadan, in the midst of the forest, and it is probably one of the most ghastly institutions in the Soviet Union.[13]

The Serpantinka (or Serpantinnaya) death camp was indeed the scene of mass executions continually through 1938, as the liquidation centre of the Northern Administration. It had been carefully prepared. One prisoner recalls that on a long journey,

On the way up, a little off from the road, we passed a few long and unpleasant-looking barracks. At one time those barracks had housed a road-building unit, and were called Serpantinnaya, but since the completion of the road to Khatenakh they had been empty for over a year. I recalled that a few days before, by orders from Magadan, Serpantinnaya had been transferred to the district section of the NKVD, which sent two brigades of men there to carry out some secret work. The little camp was to be fenced with three rows of barbed wire, watchtowers for sentries were to be erected every 25 yards, and a commodious house for officials and guards would be built as well as a garage. What puzzled me was the garage. It was not usual to build a garage in a small camp like this, especially since only three miles away were the big garages in the Khatenakh camp and in the Vodopyanov gold mines. Later I learned it was used to house two tractors, the engines of which produced enough noise to deaden the sounds of shooting and cries of the men. However, after a short stay, the tractors were moved to some gold field, and the automobile drivers who passed the camp at night sometimes heard the proceedings there with the utmost clarity.[23]

Another account tells us that, 'At Serpantinka each day thirty to fifty people were shot in a shed near the cooler. The corpses were then dragged behind a mound on motorised sledges. . . . There was also another method: prisoners were led with eyes bound to a deep trench and were shot in the ear or the back of the neck.'[32]

Serpantinka victims sometimes waited several days to be shot, standing in a shed packed so tight that when they were given a drink—in the form of pieces of ice being thrown in to them—they could not move their hands for it and had to try to catch it in their mouths.[32]

Another prisoner describes a particular case of an acquaintance:

Skeletons, they worked badly. Dyukov (the brigade leader) asked for better rations. The director refused. The famished gang tried heroically to fulfil the norms and faded away. Everyone turned against Dyukov. . . . Dyukov made more and more vigorous complaints and protests. His gang's output went on falling, and so its rations went down. Dyukov tried to intercede with the administration. This in turn asked the competent services to inscribe Dyukov and his men on the 'lists'. They shot Dyukov and all his gang one morning by the Serpantinka.[28]

Only a few fortunate prisoners, who were sentenced merely to a ten-year addition to their term, came back from Serpantinka to the camps. 'Years later they were so gripped by the horror of it that they did not dare to tell their fellow prisoners of the inhumanity they had seen and experienced. When they at last brought themselves to speak of it, they looked anxiously around to make sure that no informer was near by.'[13]

When, in the natural course of events, Garanin was himself executed the following year—apparently, like Berzin, as a 'Japanese spy'—his Serpantinka subordinates down to rank-and-file executioners, drivers and grave-diggers were shot too and the camp was razed. His victims, however, were not rehabilitated and none of his sentences was quashed. Later gold was found on the site, and had to be dug up through a veritable stratum of bones.

Serpantinka-type operations are estimated to have seen about 26,000 executions in 1938. The remainder of the 40,000 or more who (according to Roy Medvedev) were shot over the whole region during that year, perished near their own camps or at other regional centres.

Many more, probably between five and ten times as many, simply died of hunger, cold and overwork:

Since the summer of 1938, that summer of unhallowed memory, there were three degrees of punishment in the camps of the Northern Administration. The highest was shooting; the second—almost equivalent—was exile to the Shturmovoy mine, to the separate camp at Panning Unit No. 8; the third and mildest, imprisonment in the local punishment cell at the camp where the culprit lived.

It was rumoured about the Eighth Unit at Shturmovoy that no one could survive the regime there for more than a month, and that even more people passed through this camp than through the butcher shop at Serpantinnaya.[23]

A lorry driver tells that at Shturmovoy,

The tents were full of gaping holes through which blew the cold winter air. The broken iron stoves were not lit. The filth was unbelievable. The beds had neither mattresses, blankets, nor pillows. Only here and there dirty rags lay strewn about.

Seeing that there was nothing to choose from, since all tents were the same, I went into one of them and began to pace from corner to corner, to warm myself a little. I paced for a long time. . . .

It had been long dark when the men returned from work. They brought some firewood and the stoves belched forth smoke from all their holes, creating an illusion of warmth. The tents were lighted only by the fire in the stove—there were no lamps. Only the yard was lit by the dazzling searchlights set up in the watchtowers.

I had seen a great variety of men during my stay at Tumanny, among them many like those who sat around the stove in the smoke-filled tent, but I had never seen such a complete collection of typical *dokhodyagas* ['goners'].[23]

But even in the ordinary camps,

Even in the early weeks of the brief Kolyma summer, the men revealed a tendency to die at a rate never before known in the region. Frequently this happened all of a sudden, sometimes even while the man was at work. A man pushing a wheelbarrow up the high runway to the panning apparatus would suddenly halt, sway for a moment, and fall down from a height of 24 to 30 feet. And that was the end. Or a man loading a barrow, prodded by the shouts of a foreman or a guard, unexpectedly would sink to the ground, blood would gush from his mouth—and everything was over.

The death rate was particularly high among men brought to the Kolyma during the last six months. Their body resistance had been undermined in jail before they were shipped to the gold fields, and they simply succumbed under the violent pace of work.[23]

Shalamov describes how in his camp, similarly,

In the whole of 1937 only two men out of two or three thousand, one prisoner and one free man, had died in the Partisan mine. They buried them side by side under a hill. Two rough monuments, a rather smaller one for the prisoner, marked their two tombs. . . . But in 1938 an entire brigade worked permanently digging graves.

The rock and the eternally frozen earth of the permafrost refused the corpses. The rock had to be dynamited, broken open, prised apart. Digging graves involved the same procedure, the same instruments, the same material and the same workers as digging for gold. The whole brigade filled its days making these graves, or rather, ditches into which the anonymous corpses were fraternally piled—not totally anonymous perhaps, since following instructions the sub-boss representing the administration attached a tag carrying the number of his personal case to the left leg of the naked corpse before burial. . . .

The doctors did not dare in their reports to give the real cause of death. There burgeoned 'polyvitaminoses', 'pellagra', 'EPE': the enigmatic EPE was 'extreme physiological debilitation', a diagnosis which represented a step towards the truth. But only the boldest doctors, not themselves prisoners, gave such diagnoses. The formula 'alimentary dystrophy' slipped later into the reports of the Kolyma doctors, after the blockade of Leningrad during the war when it became possible to name, even though only in Latin, the true cause of death.[28]

At the same time, a new category of imprisonment was introduced—*katorga*. The word, referring to the old Tsarist system of forced labour, was in fact far worse. The *katorzhniki* worked in special camps, in chains, and without blankets or mattresses at nights. None survived.

The 'tempest' of 1938 was the worst time of all in Kolyma. Though things improved a little the following year, the principles established in 1938 remained in force. The appalling ration scales, the ban on warm clothes and shoes, a death rate lower than that of 1938 but still murderously high, marked the whole period.

As in the rest of the country, 1938 represented a violent breaking with old standards. It was followed by, and it constituted the foundation stone of, a less ravaging but in a sense an even more dehumanising consolidation and systematisation of permanent terror. There was a marked lessening in indiscriminate shooting: but that sanction remained, and was enforced frequently enough when it was thought suitable. The basic attitude of the authorities to the prisoners' life—that it was in effect already forfeit—remained firm.

In the winter of 1938–9, a prisoner tells us:

Things became somewhat calmer. There were scarcely any shootings now, but the mortality rate did not diminish since the physical resistance of the prisoners, undermined by the difficult spring and summer, now disappeared entirely under the hard winter conditions. It must also be added that the diet of the workers deteriorated dreadfully with the end of the large-scale washing. 'There is no gold, so they give us no food,' I was told by an acquaintance, an employee of the local Supply Section.[23]

One of the new orders was that work, which had hitherto stopped when the temperature went down to −50°, would go on until it was −60°. However, no thermometer was visible to the prisoners and instructions were simply phoned down by the administration. Only three working days were cancelled for reasons of low temperature in the winter of 1938–9 as against fifteen the previous winter, but even then the woodcutting workers had to go out.

The continuity of the official attitude to the prisoners can best be documented at this point by a brief selection of incidents and developments spanning the whole period.

Mrs Ginzburg recalls the fate of a friend in the winter of 1939–40:

One of us found a fairly recent number of *Pravda*, and when we read it after lights-out, its contents caused a sensation, for it gave the full text of Hitler's latest speech followed by a respectful commentary and a two-page photograph of Molotov receiving Von Ribbentrop.

'A charming family group!' remarked Katya Rotmis-trovskaya, as she climbed on to her upper bunk. She was rash. I had warned her repeatedly that there were people among us who listened carefully to what was said at night. In the end, Katya's lack of prudence cost her her life. Six months later she was shot for 'anti-Soviet propaganda in the huts'.[4]

In 1940, a Pole tells us,

The orchestra very often played while the prisoners were at work. To the accompaniment of this music, the guards would fall out prisoners whose work was especially feeble and shoot them, there and then. The shots rang out one after another. The bodies of the murdered men were also buried under the brushwood on the surface of the mines.

A Jew from Lwów working alongside me was so exhausted that he repeatedly fainted at work. The guard ordered him to fall out, took him to a near-by shed, and there he was shot. I heard the shot and saw his body a few minutes later.[2]

In the summer of 1940, Shalamov tells us of the local 'mobile detachment' designed to catch escapers. It was commanded by the young Corporal Postnikov.

Drunk with murder he fulfilled his task with zeal and passion. He had personally captured five men. As always in such cases he had been decorated and received a premium. The reward was the same for the dead and the living. It was not necessary to deliver the prisoners complete.

One August morning a man who was going to drink at a stream fell into an ambush set by Postnikov and his soldiers. Postnikov shot him down with a revolver. They decided not to drag the body to the camp but to leave it in the taiga. The signs of bears and wolves were numerous.

For identification, Postnikov cut off the fugitive's hands with an axe. He put the hands in his knapsack and went to make his report on the hunt. The report went out the same day. One soldier carried the packet. Postnikov gave leave to the others in honour of the occasion. . . . In the night the corpse got up. Pressing his bleeding wrists against his chest, he left the taiga following the trail and reached the prisoners' tent. With pale face, mad blue eyes, he looked inside, holding himself at the opening, leaning against the door posts and muttering something. Fever devoured him. His padded coat, his trousers, his rubber boots were stained with black blood.

They gave him warm soup, wrapped his chopped-off

wrists in rags and took him to the infirmary. But already Postnikov and his men came running out of their little hut. The soldiers took the prisoner. He was not heard of again. . . .[28]

Mrs Ginzburg recounts, in the same year, a refrain we shall meet again: 'We stood about for some time by the camp gates while our guards argued with Kucherenko, a big copper-faced man in charge of the infirmary and politely called "doctor", but in fact only a medical orderly. We heard him say: "*What if some of them die on the way? They're politicals.* You can see how they are dressed." As usual, our clothes were the worst of any.'[4]

In 1940 or early 1941, a free sailor at Nagayevo saw the following incident. Boxes of tinned and bottled food were being unloaded from a steamer. One fell and broke open. A bottle of preserved fruit was smashed. The stevedore bent down, picked up a piece of pear or some other fruit and put it in his mouth. The NKVD man on guard went up to him without a word and with a shot from his revolver laid him out on the spot. 'That is the rule', the sailor comments, 'for theft while loading—murder on the spot—even if the theft is of the kind described in this case. Nevertheless there is a great deal of stealing. . . . Life in any case is worth nothing. . . .'[33]

In 1941, on the outbreak of war, prisoners sentenced under Article 58 were sent from Magadan to camps in the interior; the official ten-hour working day was raised to twelve—and less officially was often sixteen; and no holidays of any sort permitted. The bread ration was fatally reduced from a kilo to half a kilo. Non-fulfilment of norms was treated as ruthlessly as in 1938, as sabotage, involving the death penalty. Sentences (signed at the time by Colonel Drabkin) were hung in the eating rooms.

All accounts of this period show it to have been

particularly lethal. But when the war ended, and more normal conditions were restored, the basic attitude remained.

In 1949, a camp doctor called Major Vostokov told one prisoner, 'Before being a doctor, I am a *chekist*, and as such I must tell you that you are not brought here to live but to suffer and die. If you live . . . it means that you are guilty of one of two things: either you worked less than was assigned you or you ate more than your proper due.'[31]

In 1950, after the first Communist defeats in Korea, a new wave of terror swept Kolyma: officials, or some of them, seemed genuinely to fear a general war and the arrival of the Americans. One prisoner reports being harangued to the effect that if the Allies did indeed land 'we shall blow up the mine entrances and you will die like rats, 200 yards below without seeing a single American or British uniform.'[31]

Orders came to carry out mass shootings for the slightest slowdown. Camp commandants had a free hand. Some shot prisoners at random, simply to spread terror. Prisoners who after fourteen hours in the mines could not do further work, were shot and their bodies left on the ground for a day as a warning. Food became worse and scarcer, the output went down, and execution for sabotage became common. And we are told, for example, that at Debin, in 1951, three prisoners of a group which had been allowed out to gather berries got lost. When they were found their heads were bashed in with rifle butts, and the camp chief, Senior Lieutenant Lomaga, had their bodies hauled past the assembled inmates in that condition.[32]

When this particular wave of terror passed, normal terror was resumed. And the continuing attitude reported by Mrs Ginzburg in 1939 was still expressed openly: 'More than once, one of the officers told us contemptuously: "If you think that we are so anxious to get more metal that we will do all in our power to keep you alive, you're mistaken! We don't give a damn for your output or your lives. All we want is to punish you for your crimes!" '[31]

Even accounts of Kolyma in 1953 show no real improvement in conditions. But the prisoners' morale naturally rose with Stalin's death and the fall of Beria, while the administration was shaken and became a trifle uncertain for the same reasons.

The immediate post-Stalin amnesty only affected prisoners doing less than five years, so applied almost entirely to common criminals. In one camp, only 2 out of 250 prisoners benefited by the amnesty.

Symbolic changes in the camp included a cancellation of the rule requiring prisoners to wear numbers on their clothing, and from then on they were called by their names. In one camp, the commandant, a Colonel Vasiliev, commonly known as 'the Rat', who a month previously 'would have beaten a prisoner to death as a matter of routine if he had caught him without a number', delivered a strange harangue to his charges, lasting more than an hour, beginning with the revolt of Spartacus and ending by threatening severe punishment to anyone caught wearing a number. He concluded, 'Woe to those who misunderstand our deeds and mistake our humanitarian feelings for weakness! They will be summarily wiped out.'[31]

It was only in 1955–6 that we can really speak of the system coming to an end, or at least becoming far smaller, less arbitrary, and with a much lower death rate. The days when Kolyma was one end of the spectrum typifying Stalinism, with the Lubyanka at the other, had ended, and only the labour camp system as it persists today remained.

When we deal, in the chapters that follow, with every aspect of Kolyma, we shall see that the accounts vary little, even as concerns quite minor detail, whether they are dated from 1939 or 1943 or 1948 or 1952.

We have in this chapter dealt briefly with the frightful actions and the inhumane habits of mind on which, from 1938, the Kolyma system proper was built, and sketched the persistence of that tradition. As we said, there were to be ups and downs, 'good' years and bad. The differences are worth recording. But they were no more than minor variations in a consistent pattern, in the established order of things in the Kolyma which we shall be describing.

Over the whole period, the ruling principle of Kolyma was that expressed in the brief and well-remembered address which the post-war Head of Dalstroy, General Derevenko, used to greet the newly arrived drafts as they fell in in fives at Nagayevo: 'Convicts! This is Kolyma! The law is the taiga, and the public prosecutor is the bear! Never expect to eat soup and bread together. What comes first, eat first! What's gone from your hands is lost for ever. You are here to work, and to work hard! You must repay with your sweat and tears the crimes perpetrated against the Soviet State and the Soviet people! No tricks, no monkey business. We are fair with those who co-operate, pitiless with those who don't. We need metal, and you must produce this metal according to The Plan. The fulfilment of The Plan is our sacred duty. Those who do not fulfil The Plan are saboteurs and traitors, and we show them no mercy!'[31]

CHAPTER FOUR

THE SOCIAL ORDER OF KOLYMA

In Kolyma a whole new social order in microcosm arose, with not only a formal and official structure, but also a network of economic and other relationships and customs, together with the growth of deep-set habits of mind appropriate to the society which gave them birth.

This Kolyma social system reflected, in exaggerated form, the new nexus of privilege, power, exploitation and subordination which had come into being throughout the USSR. At the pinnacle of the Kolyma 'new class' came, of course, the Head of Dalstroy—a potentate whose word was law throughout the vast territories of the North-East.* We can easily set out the handful of other families who constituted the *crème de la crème*: they were those who had the privilege of shopping in the special store, already one of the perquisites of the Stalinist élite throughout the Soviet Union, which remains to this day one of the great economic benefits awarded to the privilegentsia. At Magadan this was

---

* The area was once visited—at a time in 1952 when a nuclear plant was planned to use the recently discovered uranium deposits—by a man even more powerful than the Head of Dalstroy. This was Beria's close associate General Goglidze, who terrified everybody, both official and prisoner. He was at this time Head of the Secret Police for the whole of the Far East. His execution the following year was welcomed by all.

known as the Devyatka, or 'Niner'. Only nine families held the special pass which procured them, even in wartime, every luxury from oranges to chocolate to fine shoes and American cigarettes. These were:

1. The Head of Dalstroy
2. His deputy, the Head of USVITL
3. The Head of the Political Administration
4. The Head of Procurement
5. The Head of the NKVD Troops in Kolyma
6. The Head of the Guard Troops in Kolyma
7. The Head of the Regular Troops in Kolyma
8. The Head of the Economic Department
9. The Head of the Health Department for all Dalstroy[13]

Below these, in an intricate pecking order beset with endless petty struggles for advantage, came first their official subordinates, according to rank; then the free specialists; then the *urkas*; and finally the 'political' prisoners.

The successive heads of Dalstroy were, particularly in their position of comparative isolation from the rest of the USSR, men of power—responsible satraps of the most distant and detached province of the Stalin empire. They normally ranked high. Nikishov was not merely a member of the Supreme Soviet, but actually a (candidate) member of the Central Committee itself, a colleague of Kosygin, Suslov and the others. It is true that they were subject to the usual precariousness of high position under despotism; but so were members of the Politburo itself. Meanwhile, they enjoyed the fruits.

Nikishov in 1942, at the age of fifty, divorced his first wife and married a Young Communist of twenty-nine named Gridassova, a primitive, crude, avaricious creature, Mrs Lipper tells us, 'who was only too well known to myself and to other female prisoners, for she functioned as the harsh commander of the Magadan women's camp.' Thanks to her husband's position she rose in the military hierarchy and was decorated. She became the Head of Maglag, the camp district of Magadan and the surrounding region, and ruled the lives of tens of thousands of prisoners.

The couple's country house forty-five miles north-west of Magadan was furnished and equipped in the greatest comfort and was surrounded by Nikishov's private hunting preserve. 'Nearby the prisoners of the invalid camp called "Seventy-second Kilometre" worked in a glass factory which was under the special protection of Gridassova and consequently always registered a marvellous production record. During the war burnt-out electric bulbs were repaired there, since new bulbs were almost unobtainable and even tiny bulbs were sold at 150 roubles.'[13]

The Derevenkos, who succeeded the Nikishovs, also lived like princes. Derevenko

organised his own theatre, had his own court artists, wrestlers, clowns, and so on. When sea traffic opened he would fly from Magadan to Vanino in his own plane, along with his artistic advisers, and select from the tens of thousands of unfortunates a handful of prisoners considered good enough by Captain Ziger, his first counsellor, to join his personal theatre company. Ostensibly this theatrical company was to distract his overworked mind from his heavy state responsibilities. For those few actors and artists, life was different from that of the other prisoners. They lived in town, had a few amenities, performed on the stage, and went around in two big American Diamond-T trucks to play before camp inmates. Derevenko's prisoner troupe toured the labour camps in the entire north-eastern tip of Siberia, visiting each camp about once a month. This was no amateur group. It included numerous professionals who had not only performed at the Bolshoi, but on the main stages of Europe. They travelled with reasonably good costumes and sets. Derevenko . . . charged each prisoner 15 roubles admission per performance. Obviously none of the prisoners had that kind of money. But the regime provided an allowance for each prisoner, the allowance to be retained by camp authorities until the day of release—when regulations stipulated that the prisoner was to receive 300 roubles 'liberation money'. The 15 roubles we paid for these shows were deducted from this special fund and pocketed by Derevenko.

Derevenko and his advisers watched the arrival of our *etap* with keen interest. From it they selected some outstanding performers—a former dancer of the Tbilisi Opera, a violinist from Shanghai, an actress from Moscow and another from Berlin, a famous trumpet-player, Eddy Rosner, and his four-piece band. They were all given a bath, fresh clothes, and promptly sent by special plane to Magadan where they were to start performing for the enjoyment of Derevenko and his wife.

Derevenko's wife, Galina Efimovna,

had acquired the airs and graces of a person of stature and not only wanted to be recognised as such, but to be unanimously accepted as the 'First Lady' of the region. She was a huge woman, weighing about 250 pounds, and resembled her husband in many ways. Though rude and arrogant, she still had her femininity. She liked to dress according to the latest Paris fashions, which meant that she kept the camp seamstresses and dressmakers working day and night '*par amour pour le Roi de Prusse*'.

A Romanian shoemaker once showed me the white brocade ball shoes he was making for her, carefully covering the delicate material with a white cloth so as not to get the slightest spot on it.[31]

And so it was, in varying degrees of self-indulgence, in the lower leadership.

Any lady who had the slightest connection with the camp administration would have her coats made free in the prisoners' tailor shops. For their private benefit camp commanders freely made use of prisoners as cobblers, tailors, painters, artisans, fishermen, doctors, and so on. With the co-operation of prisoners in charge of food supplies and prisoners in charge of book-keeping all sorts of manipulations were carried on. The prisoners had every incentive to co-operate. It ensured their hold on the comfortable jobs, and they made a little profit besides; the mass of the prisoners in the camp suffered.[13]

In the Berelyakh camp group its chief, Colonel Vasiliev, exploited anyone who came within his range. Every day, a party of no less than 25 girls had to go to work at his house—milking the cows, feeding the hens, and polishing the furniture. Everything had to be done, of course, without pay. . . . All services and supplies came to him entirely free of charge. . . .

One day he ordered the camp's carpentry shop to produce a complete classroom [for his son]—blackboards, desks and all. The cabinet-makers were told to use the best materials and the best of workmanship. They did an excellent job with some first-class carving, and they were very proud of their product. The problem now was the price. They knew full well what a stingy, miserable man Vasiliev was. But they had to account for the costly materials used. After much scratching of heads, they decided to quote him a price that barely covered the cost of the raw materials involved. They sent the bill to the camp's head office where it eventually reached the Colonel's desk.

Next morning 'the Rat' burst into the workshop and began to curse the squad leader and his cabinet-makers, calling them thieves and robbers.

'Don't you believe in God?' he ranted. 'How can you try to rob me? I am a poor working man, striving hard for my daily bread! How can you charge me eight hundred roubles!'

The frightened squad leader, anxious to soothe the Colonel's anger, told him: 'Citizen Colonel, there has been a gross mistake. That bill was not for you, but meant for someone else. We'll send your bill along tomorrow.'

The following day, Colonel Vasiliev found on his desk a new bill for only 300 roubles. It didn't cover a third of the cost of the raw materials, but he was quite satisfied because no one would accuse *him* of damaging the interests of the State.[31]

A woman hospital chief, who owed her position to having married a prominent NKVD officer, is described by Mrs Lipper:

She had the manner of a lazy, well-fed cat. She never raised her somewhat nasal, eternally bored voice, not even when she sent an orderly to the gold mines for some minor offence.

She came fully awake only when she talked about needlework, which she had her nurses make for her in large quantities. Patterns, yarn, colour-combinations were the things that passionately interested her. Nurses who did not know embroidery, no matter how conscientious they were about attending their patients, were treated by her with contemptuous tolerance; those who could do needlework could neglect their patients as much as they wished and still be sure of the favour and protection of this so-called doctor.

In the women's ward there were always a few patients who looked and were remarkably healthy. These were kept busy embroidering tablecloths and tapestry hangings—in the style of our grandmothers.

All the ladies of Magadan society were wild about this hobby and competed with one another—to the great joy of those prisoners who could do such work, for they could thereby earn additional food. It was amusing to see the wives of NKVD officers outbid one another in sending secret presents to the 'counter-revolutionaries'; officially such gifts were strictly forbidden, of course. But the ladies were so excited at the chance to enrich themselves cheaply—for in their eyes this superfluous and generally tasteless needlework represented wealth—that they forgot their ostentatious hatred and contempt for the *contriki*.[13]

Such—a handful of stories among dozens—was the life of the privileged caste. Even at a local level, Shalamov tells of the fortunes made by officials.

Time and again, one is struck by the extraordinary gap

between the ruling privilegentsia and the prisoners. Even in Berzin's time, when the camp administration were

pretty decent men or, at any rate, not vicious ones, one thing was characteristic of them all: they did not regard the prisoners who were in their charge and dependent on them as quite human, although some of them had been in the very same shoes in the past. Their attitude towards persons who had lost their freedom was very similar to that of the whites toward the Negroes in the United States during the period described in *Uncle Tom's Cabin*.

This attitude had entered into the very blood of these men, for almost unlimited power over living beings, deprived of nearly every right, inevitably awakens the specific instincts of arbitrary tyranny, absolute intolerance of any opposition from these 'lower creatures', and complete irresponsibility in dealing with them. True, the illiterate fool Brukhnov was proud of having at his command and working as common miners eighteen professors. But his pride grew out of his awareness that all these people, better and more intelligent and more honest than he—the flower of the nation—were in his hands, while he, a fool who could not write his own name, could exercise his power over them at will, in any form and with total impunity.[23]

Or again, we are told that Sukhanov, then Head of the Northern Administration, had a servant who had formerly been a professor of psychiatry. He treated him well, but with a certain contemptuousness which even the best of free employees seemed unable to escape in their relations with prisoners.

In the 1940s this attitude was to be found everywhere:

At twenty-eight Nina Vladimirovna was the head of a hospital for 500 patients, which she always spoke of as 'my' hospital. She behaved like a *pomeshchitsa*, a great lady and landowner of Tsarist times, and considered the entire staff of the hospital her personal serfs. . . .
She felt neither hatred nor contempt for the prisoners, no

more than a landowner of earlier times would have hated his serfs. She looked upon them as tools supplied by nature to increase her wealth, as the prerequisites for her position of power. But she was able to pity them.[13]

In a rather different context, we again find even women and doctors sharing the slave-owner mentality—already noted at Vanino and Nakhodka—at the Magadan transit camp (in 1949):

We were paraded naked in front of a medical board of young girl internes just out from the Moscow University Medical School. Then we were carefully examined by broad-shouldered unfriendly-looking civilians dressed in sheepskin coats and wearing high felt boots. These were the mine managers, the representatives of the Ministry of Internal Affairs, the owner and sole supplier of detainee manpower. They pinched our muscles, opened our jaws, and felt our teeth. If satisfied, they addressed the board with the words, 'I take him.' There was seldom any protest from the medical beauties who examined us with regard to the health of the man thus chosen. They merely nodded, an entry was ticked off, and the man's fate was sealed. He was headed for one of the mines.[31]

At a lower level, the free specialists and others often lived more squalidly, while yet finding themselves in economic and other connection with the prisoners who lived incomparably more squalidly still. The atmosphere of social distinction was so pervasive that it affected even the very young. One Russian victim describes free children enjoying themselves by throwing stones at women prisoners.[34]

In 1940 the hotel in Magadan was a large grey barrack, containing middle officials waiting for their houses to be built, alcoholic mining clerks, 'pickpockets plying their trade between two sentences; and even a few forgers who, in spite of lack of tools, managed to make passable identity cards'. In the hotel, where 'mining engineers, prostitutes and the bosses of Kolyma got drunk on pure alcohol, fornicated, stole and cursed',[4] scrubbing the floors was nevertheless a joy and a privilege for the women prisoners, who even met kindness from some of the inhabitants, though also having to foil rape attempts and prostitution offers.

There were other forms of connection between the lesser free population and the convicts. In the easier camps the prisoners traded not only among themselves, but with the free citizenry also. In Kolyma all goods were rationed because of transportation difficulties. The inhabitants had ration cards long before the war. Free citizens bought textiles and food at state prices and sold them at black-market prices to the prisoners. These transactions had to be managed behind the backs of the guards; but there were always opportunities for at least a few prisoners, and they then passed on the goods to the less privileged prisoners—adding their own profit to the purchase price.

In addition to genuine free citizens, there were freedmen—the handful of released prisoners, the lowest of the non-prisoner population. These two groups regarded themselves as of quite different social status and rarely mingled. (Except, that is, that no stigma attached to former women prisoners.) But most of the old free specialists were in any case re-arrested in 1937–8 even though some—especially geologists—were to be released in 1939.

Prisoners who were released were, if under fifty and not declared invalids, forbidden to leave Kolyma. So were those over fifty if their skills were urgently needed in the region—that is everyone from engineers to cooks. After the war, there was a special regulation for prisoners of German origin, including Volga Germans, German exiles and even German Jews. They had to sign an application to stay, and almost all were sent to a special community barracks in the remote area of Tyenki.

There is even one extraordinary borderline case quoted, of a prisoner who had completed his sentence and not been given another one, who was yet not issued with his discharge papers and went on working for many months with the remarkable status of 'free prisoner'.[9]

We may suitably recount here the fate of an anomalous group—one of the most extraordinary set of inmates which even Kolyma had seen.

In its earlier days the Road-Building Administration, and the settlement of Yagodnoye at which it was located, were the best-managed enterprises in Kolyma. This was due to the efficiency of the Administration's chiefs.

It was common practice under Berzin to employ skilled and experienced prisoners in important administrative and technical posts. This was the case even with quite ordinary prisoners. But the Yagodnoye men sent him in 1935–6 were a very special category. They were none other than the Leningrad NKVD officers Medved, Zaporozhets, Fomin, Yanishevsky, Mosevich, members of that group of twelve which had, on 23 January 1935, been sentenced to short terms of imprisonment for failing to observe the basic requirements of state security, in that 'having received information about the preparations for the attempt on S. M. Kirov . . . they failed to take the necessary measures to prevent the assassination . . . although they had every possible means of arresting it'.

As Khrushchev was to remark twenty years later, 'After the murder of Kirov, top functionaries of the Leningrad NKVD were given very light sentences, but in 1937 they were shot. We can assume that they were shot in order to cover the traces of the organisers of Kirov's killing.' But even at the time, the sentences struck leading circles in the NKVD as disproportionately light. Stalin would, in the natural course of events, have ordered the exemplary execution of anyone involved in a criminal failure to guard against a genuine assassination attempt. Moreover, it became known that Yagoda had ordered specially good treatment for them, sent them to their destinations not in a prison van but by special coach, and ordered his secretary to look after their families; while their former colleagues sent them presents, contrary to the strict Stalin rule of instantly breaking with friend or relations once arrested. This is not the place to give a full account of the evidence on the murder of Kirov.* It is enough to say that it seems clear that Stalin procured it through Yagoda, who worked through Zaporozhets, then Deputy Head of the Leningrad NKVD. Some recent books, even reputable ones, have taken the line that the case against Stalin is not proven. This is true in the narrow and formal sense that complete juridical 'proof' is naturally lacking. But, as Roy Medvedev, the Leninist dissident writer, has said, there can no longer be any real doubt about it. And, above all, the information available is incompatible with any other conclusion.

So here they were, with their wives, treated in all but name as powerful and prominent officials—until it became suitable for Stalin to disembarrass himself of them. But the most extraordinary part of the story, as far as Kolyma is concerned, is that after the other Leningrad policemen had been re-arrested and taken to Moscow, Zaporozhets himself remained for some time at his post, a lone exception. He is reported as still in charge of the Road-Building Administration and resisting the transfer of his headquarters from Yagodnoye months after his colleagues had disappeared. —Presumably the announcement on 2 March 1938, in connection with the Bukharin trial, that he had organised Kirov's death on Yagoda's orders and that he was being made 'the subject of separate proceedings', marks his

* See *The Great Terror* by Robert Conquest chapter V (London and New York: Macmillan, 1968, 1973).

77

final disappearance. (Yagoda's instructions, passed on to Zaporozhets, were now alleged to have been given by Abel Yenukidze—who has, however, long since been rehabilitated and who, even at the time, was clearly not in a position to give instructions to the Head of the Secret Police, who took his orders from one man only.)

Thus, in spite of the sharp polarisation of Kolyma society between the privilegentsia and the prisoners, there was—as is indeed not uncommon in such societies—an intermediate stratum. There were free men who were scarcely better than prisoners, even occasional prisoners who ranked higher than some free citizens. The social order was a complex one. Still, the basic division remained clear and the moral and social corruption of the system is evident.

Nevertheless, it is worth noting that, as we have said, instances of actual humanity to prisoners were occasionally to be found, even after 1937. These usually led to trouble. We are told (*Literaturnaya Gazeta*, 4 April 1964) of a geologist who intervened on humanitarian grounds. He once complained to an official:

'These people might die!'

'What people?' The representative of the Camp Administration smiled. 'These are enemies of the people.'

As a result the geologist himself lost his life.

The only solidarity of this sort which really helped, and of which there are many examples, is when free specialists such as doctors and engineers tried and sometimes succeeded in getting prisoners with qualifications suitable posts: almost all the witnesses we quote only survived, as we shall see, as the result of getting office or nursing jobs, and not seldom by these means.

The hierarchical structure of Kolyma society applied not only as between free men and prisoners, but also among the prisoners themselves.

First came the *urkas* who ranked, in the social scale of Kolyma, far above the lowest of the low, the 'politicals'. Hitherto, the politicals had been terrorised by the *urkas*, on the ship or earlier, in spontaneous acts of robbery and violence. They were now to find this oppression consciously taken advantage of by the authorities, and built into the system. Officialdom made it clear to the *urkas* that they were a privileged stratum. A former criminal is quoted by Roy Medvedev: 'They tried to let us know that we thieves were still not lost to the homeland; prodigal, so to speak, but nevertheless sons. But for "fascists" and "counters" (i.e. politicals) there was no place on this mortal earth and never would be in all ages to come. . . . And if we were thieves, then our place was beside the stove, while "phrase-mongers" and all that sort had their place by the doors and in the corners.'[16]

They exploited this support ruthlessly. Roy Medvedev holds that the Stalin technique of putting criminals and politicals together 'was no better or worse than the idea of creating gas ovens in Auschwitz'. Whatever we may think of that particular comparison, it is certainly true that it was a conscious decision, under which the already starving and terrorised politicals found their inadequate rations, their meagre clothing, and their lives constantly at the mercy of capricious and conscienceless thugs to whom murder meant little, theft less.

We have described the strange subhuman culture of the *urka* world. Their speech was a strange jargon, with an amazingly continuous obscenity—(found, indeed, also among the administration, even at the highest level). Their bodies, too, were usually distinguishable from those of politicals by thick tattooing. Even their women were sometimes indelibly disfigured in this way, often in a manner described as incredibly obscene.

Urkas had one weakness, reported time and again in our

sources. They loved to listen to stories. That is to say, not anecdotes, but, for example, the whole length of *The Count of Monte Cristo*, and as far as possible in the original words. This was true even of those who knew the story well already: they preferred to hear it told in an 'educated' voice and manner. Time and again politicals were not only saved from beating or murder, but actually fed and helped for this one talent. 'The only privileged political prisoner' (as Mrs Ginzburg puts it) 'was the one who could tell stories or who could give a verbal rendition of some adventurous novel.'[4]

But the normal relationship of the *urkas* to the politicals was different. First of all, they got all the easier posts and a disproportionate share of the food, with the result, as Shalamov notes, that 'At the mine, we only got half the rations, the rest having fallen off en route into the plates of the bosses, the staff and the common criminals.'[28]

General Gorbatov, writing of a Maldyak camp where there were 400 politicals and 50 *urkas*, describes how the theft was formalised:

'The enemies of the people', as a rule, were detailed for the heaviest jobs, the lighter work being given to the 'trusties' or common criminals. . . . It was they who were appointed foremen, cooks, orderlies and tent seniors. Naturally enough the small amounts of fat released for the pot chiefly found their way into the bellies of the 'trusties'. There were three types of rations: one for those who had not fulfilled their quota, another for those who had, and a third for those who had exceeded their quota. The latter automatically included the 'trusties'. They did little enough work, but the tally clerks were of their persuasion and so they swindled, putting to their own and their mates' credit the work that we had done. As a result the criminals fed well and the politicals went hungry.[5]

It is even the case that the authorities went out of their way to select men with particularly bad records for overseer jobs. Gorbatov mentions a curious case: 'Boris was nick-named "the Careerist". He got this name in one of the northern camps because he made himself out to be a big criminal, with six murders and five major robberies to his credit. He was believed, and was appointed a senior prisoner. Then it turned out that he was simply an independant, small-time thief. There was a great fuss and he was demoted and given his nickname.'[5]

Criminals were favoured in other ways. Out of the mass of criminals in Kolyma, a few hundred would be picked out and released shortly before their term was up.

The list of the names of these people, who were called 200-per-centers (*dvukhsotniki*), was posted in the dining rooms of all the camps, so that the rest would learn from the example of these super-producers. On closer examination you discovered to your surprise that a prisoner who had worked as a chambermaid for some NKVD chief was listed as a 200-per-center in woodcutting, for which meritorious accomplishment she was being released before completion of her sentence. Most of these people were criminals who had distinguished themselves in the service of the camp authorities by special cruelty towards their fellow prisoners, and who were falsely listed as miners; or else they were brigadiers who had made a name for themselves by denunciations and ruthless driving of their workers.[13]

In addition to the regular and legalised theft of food, ordinary robbery, often with violence, went on unchecked. Shalamov tells a typical story:

One day—an exceptional event since they arrived very rarely—I got a parcel: airman's boots made of felt. Our relatives did not understand our conditions of life. . . . They would have been stolen the first night. So, even before leaving the office with the commandant, I sold them for 100 roubles to the team boss, Andrei Boyko. The boots were worth 700 roubles but it was a good sale. I had the means to buy 100 kilograms of bread or perhaps butter and sugar. I hadn't eaten any butter or sugar since my stay in prison. At the shop I bought a kilo of butter—41 roubles. As soon as this purchase was made—in the middle of the day, as we were working at night—I ran to Sheinin, who lived in another barracks, to celebrate. I had also bought some bread.

Emotion and joy made Sheinin stutter: 'But I haven't the right! Why me?' he murmured, overwhelmed. 'No, I can't.' I finally convinced him and he went off running to get some hot water. Immediately a terrible blow on the neck sent me rolling to the ground. When I got up the bag of bread and butter had disappeared. The great chunk of wood with which I'd been knocked out lay by a mattress. Around me everyone was laughing. Sheinin arrived with a pot of hot water. . . .[28]

Sometimes the motives were different: 'On his first night in camp they stole a Dutch Communist's shirt and the photograph of his wife. Every time I remembered this I felt worried and embarrassed. Who could need the photo of a foreign woman and why? "You don't see?" a grinning colleague said to me one day. "It's not difficult to guess, some toughs pinched the photo, to organise, as they say, seances of masturbation.'[28]

Robbery extended to the products of work, where possible:

Sometimes it happened that we and the criminals were sent off for wood together. We, the 'enemies of the people', would go into the forest; the criminals would lie in wait for us not far from the camp. As we came back they would grab our load and, if they were feeling generous, say: 'We'll help you carry that.' We were forbidden to return to camp without any wood and so back we had to go for more, a couple of miles into the forest. Sometimes things went even worse, depending on who happened to come your way. You might be attacked and have your load snatched from you, and you might be badly beaten up, for good measure, and told: 'You're a Communist, aren't you? You defended Soviet power, didn't you? Well, here's your thanks . . .'[5]

But more basically, this regime of violence was, as we have said, harnessed to the official machine, with the *urkas* acting as supervisors of the 'political' serfs.

'The *urkas* did not work. With their clubs—their "thermometers" as they laughingly called them—in hand, they strode among the diggings to ensure the execution of The Plan. They threw themselves on the defenceless politicals, and often beat them to death. —"Politicals" . . . unbridled repression against millions had put under this title innocent men of all politics. . . . They were martyrs but not heroes.'[28]

A Romanian prisoner gives a fairly typical specific instance:

After twelve hours work that first day, we began to climb down the slippery path to our camp quarters. My heart was pounding, my limbs were stiff and aching. My whole body was in such a state of exhaustion that I felt certain that a few more days of such hard labour would finish me. As we slid down the slope like a bunch of drunks, the brigade leader stopped us in front of a barn-like building from which a weak beam of light shone out into the pitch-dark night.

'Halt!' he said. 'I want everybody to go in and bring out two cement bags to load the truck.'

Inside, in a dusty, choking atmosphere, people began to load the bags on their shoulders and haul them out to be loaded on a waiting truck. With some help I lifted up the two bags on my back and, bending under their weight, directed my feet towards the door. Whether it was my state of exhaustion after the exhausting day's work, or whether I slipped on the threshold, I still don't know, but I fell on my back and the cement bags flew from me. One of the bags burst open and the contents spilled all over. I heard shouts and curses, but I couldn't stand up.

At that moment the brigade leader arrived on the scene

and began to beat me with a thick iron rod, calling me all sorts of names. The blows were falling indiscriminately all over me, and I felt certain that the next one would finish me. But I still could not make it to my feet. Finally, his thirst for blood satisfied, he allowed some of my fellow inmates to help me back on my feet. I tried to move, convinced that death was round the corner. I don't know how I eventually reached the camp. I needed immediate medical attention, but there was no doctor in the male barracks. The nearest medical officer was in the women's camp, and one could only go there with the permission of the camp officials.

I had to face the danger that the brigade leader would find out that I had sought a doctor and would kill me on the spot in his fury. After all, justice was on his side. I took the risk and went to the woman doctor.[31]

Even this was a comparatively mild case, since the prisoner survived. All accounts have reports in which 'Innocent people were savagely beheaded with axes in broad daylight or stabbed to death with picks and shovels. . . .'[31]

One typical *urka* atrocity was to break the bones of the victim, lifting him by his hands and legs and throwing his body violently on the ground. 'The victim would groan and plead for mercy, but nobody would listen. When, after twenty or thirty such vicious throws, the victim finally remained silent, the criminals would simply leave him there and proceed to report their deed to the authorities. And so the cycle went: a mock trial, an added sentence, and then back for more violence, brutality, and murder.'[31]

As we saw on the ships, the *urkas* also submitted their own kind to a savage discipline, if their code was seen to be broken. An *urka* at the Ola camp, Alexei, nicknamed 'Stumpy',

had three fingers missing from his left hand. He was generally morose and taciturn but once, not without great difficulty, he managed to get out: 'I've done two big jobs myself. One was with one murder. The second one I did three people in.'

I asked him how he had lost his fingers. . . .

'I was playing cards and I lost. I had no cash so I staked a good suit, not mine of course, one that a political had on. I lost. I meant to take the suit during the night when the new prisoner had stripped for bed. I had to hand it over before eight in the morning, only they took the political away to another camp that very day. Our council of seniors met to hand out my punishment. The plaintiff wanted all my left-hand fingers off. The seniors offered two. They bargained a bit and agreed on three. So I put my hand on the table and the man I'd lost to took a stick and with five strokes knocked off my three fingers.'

Stumpy was quite cool about his story. He added: 'We have our laws too, only tougher than yours. If you do your comrades down you've got to answer for it.'[5]

One particular *urka* execution, carried out while at work, is said to have been the origin of a camp regulation:

They only distributed our scythes and axes in the morning before going to work. In the neighbouring brigade, a group of common criminals had recently settled accounts with their brigade leader. Always inclined towards the theatrical, the toughs, having decided to kill the brigadier, enthusiastically greeted the proposal to cut off his head. They decapitated him with an ordinary scythe. Hence the ban on leaving scythes and axes with the prisoners during the night. Why only during the night? No one questions the logic of a regulation.[28]

One 'political' describes a criminal *samosud*—*urka* court—which he witnessed. A young criminal called Sashka was charged with betraying his fellow thieves to the camp administration. Found guilty he was asked how he wanted to die, 'by cutting or by hanging'. The barrack had already seen inmates strangled to death with a sock or a sleeve, stabbed, or having their skulls split with an axe, but previously in moments of criminal rage. The cold-blooded scene which now ensued was something new to them.

Sashka chose cutting. A wash-basin was produced, he was made to kneel over it, and his throat was cut on the spot. The executioner cleaned his hands with drinking water from the barrel, kicked the body and then banged on the door to call the sentry and report the deed.[31]

For during the Stalin period, while people could be executed for anti-Soviet agitation in camp, there was no death penalty for murder. As a result, the *urkas* killed with what was, in effect, complete immunity. After even the most public and brutal murders, they would only be taken off and sentenced to a further five or ten years. And since the length of sentence meant nothing (many of them would be serving accumulated sentences of fifty or even a hundred years), this did not act as a deterrent. But in any case, even apart from legal sanctions, such murders (and particularly of politicals) hardly even brought them moral censure from the camp administration. When the death penalty was introduced for murder in 1950, there was a great falling-off of crimes of this sort.

After the war, for a time, the *urkas* became less powerful in a number of the camps. Instead of the meek 'Trotskyites' of the earlier period, the new intake consisted of hard-bitten soldiers, fully prepared to stick together and fight back, and equally tough and united Ukrainian and other nationalists. The soldiers (though not of course the nationalists) were even able to exploit the system on occasion to the extent of taking over the leading prisoner positions, traditionally reserved for the criminals.

In 1951, when a hundred thousand prisoners were packed into the Magadan transit camp, several thousand *urkas* were held in one of the fourteen separate enclosures. They broke into a *katorzhnik* section, to steal food and clothing, but the new prisoners fought back so effectively that the *urkas* decided instead to break out and loot Magadan. After killing several N.C.O.s they were repelled from the gates by machine-gun fire. In the end the death roll on all sides amounted to around 300. The survivors were sent to the Kholodnaya lead mines, a notoriously deadly site.[31]

In fact, the symbiosis of *urka* and officialdom, though effective in its main purpose of repressing the 'politicals', was never complete. The *urkas* regarded themselves as an independent society; and they were always liable to extravagant outbursts, individual or in groups, against the authorities.

Yet another stratum, officially political prisoners too, yet remained slightly better off than the rank and file. These were the informers, who were slipped extra rations, and the promise of earlier release, in exchange for denunciation.

Such denunciation was a necessary part of NKVD legalism, as witnesses were conventionally required to establish a crime and enable further sentences to be imposed. Sometimes, indeed, the NKVD would launch provocations directly.

The Secret Police also resorts to provocation whenever it has to 'formalize the liquidation' of counter-revolutionary elements who have otherwise given no ground for execution and whom it considers dangerous and deserving of such punishment.

It should be observed that although the Secret Police is not bound by any rules or laws during an investigation, it is careful, once the investigation has been finished, to formalize the juridical aspects of a case with regard to procedures and appearances, so that the case will give the impression of having been conducted in conformity with the laws of the U.S.S.R.[38]

Shalamov tells us that an automatic persecution was arranged for any prisoner who had reached the last year of his sentence, on Moscow's order, with provocations, narks' reports, interrogations. He instances one prisoner due for release who, 'so that things should be in order', is denounced, on the instructions of the authorities, by another prisoner for 'chanting the praises of Hitler'.

Elinor Lipper describes a typical attempt to mount a 'provocation' against an honest doctor prisoner. A bottle of alcohol and some poison were found in the doctor's bunk in the barracks while he and the other prisoners were away at work. It was put about that a terrorist Trotskyite organisation had been discovered. Witnesses were produced by threats and beatings. Unfortunately, the chief witness was a tough young Ukrainian who was the doctor's medical orderly. ('Ukrainians can be extremely stubborn, especially when they are serving a ten-year sentence anyway.') He proved that the doctor did not drink and could have taken all the alcohol he wanted when at work. It was then alleged that the alcohol was used to bribe accomplices.

However, things had now been held up so long that an NKVD investigative officer hostile to the commandant took over. He saw that, from his point of view, 'no political capital could be made' of the case. This would have done no good, but he turned up a fact that destroyed the whole story—that the bottle in which the poison was found was of a type used in the *provocateur's* office only. The accomplices confessed. Those concerned in the frame-up disappeared, including the camp commandant. As Mrs Lipper said, 'The incident was one of the very rare triumphs of justice in the Soviet Union, and deserves to be remembered for that reason.'[13]

In November 1937, Filimonov, Head of the Militarized Guard, organised a remarkable provocation at the Kresty fisheries camp, near Sredne-Kolymsk. He had the local guard chief tell a prisoner that orders had been given to shoot all the prisoners. A hastily organised revolt took place.

But after holding the camp for some weeks the prisoners had little choice but to surrender. Most of them seem to have been shot.[38]

The role of the regular informer is most strikingly illustrated by a figure of whom we chance to have separate reports, from Elinor Lipper and Varlam Shalamov respectively—the former Deputy People's Commissar for Heavy Industry Krivitsky (who is also mentioned, though in friendlier tones, by Mrs Ginzburg as a helpful fellow passenger on the *Dzhurma*).

A distinguished surgeon, a prisoner called Dr Koch, was the best in Magadan, and was always resorted to by the top administration. However, the free chief physician had him denounced and he was sent to the Berelyakh mines. Here, after the outbreak of war, he became particularly vulnerable, as a Volga German.

In 1943 he was accused of having made pro-Hitler, pro-fascist speeches to a group of prisoners. The shameful witness at this trial was the despicable Krivitsky, former Deputy People's Commissar for Heavy Industry, who himself had been sentenced in 1937 to fifteen years' imprisonment as a counter-revolutionary. A slimy, fawning, cunning creature, he hoped to buy his freedom by acting as a *provocateur*. Old Koch, whose sole fault was that he had saved the lives of thousands of people, was shot. . . .

In 1945, when I was working in the prisoners' hospital in the northern gold-mine region, Krivitsky was in the hospital from a stroke of paralysis. I noticed how some of the patients from Berelyakh watched him with mingled hatred and fear, and refused to have anything to do with him. I did not understand until they told me of the numerous victims of Krivitsky's informing activities.[13]

Krivitsky also features in the camp trial at which Shalamov received his second sentence, to provide the formal basis for keeping him in after he had served his first.

Shalamov speaks of the leading camp denouncers who set him up for it—Krivitsky, the former Deputy Commissar for Industry, and Zaslavsky, a journalist on *Izvestia*.* (Two witnesses were, in fact, required by regulations.)

After a month on penal rations—'300 grams of bread and a bowl of water' —to which the jailer twice added a spoonful of soup, Shalamov was ready for his interrogation. As he says, in the conflict of wills which constitutes such an interrogation, a man in his state is at a disadvantage. He adds: 'If the interrogators of Kolyma had prepared Georgy Dimitrov, the universe would never have heard of the Leipzig trials.'

The witnesses produced an accusation of sympathy towards the German offensive. Shalamov replied that, as he hadn't read a paper for six years, he knew nothing whatever about it.

Worse still, he had said that the 'Stakhanovite' movement in the camp was a cheat. And, besides, he had asserted that Bunin was a great Russian writer.

'And so he is a great Russian writer. And can I be condemned for saying that?'

'Yes, you can. He's an émigré and an enemy.'

Finally, he went before the tribunal. They had actually assembled four witnesses, one of whom however he had never even met. The only question he asked was, 'Why is it that you have the same witnesses for all the accused?' After deliberation, on 26 June 1942, he was given ten years extra.

As to his delators, he says, 'Krivitsky is dead, it seems. Zaslavsky got back to Moscow, and joined the Union of Writers, even though he'd never written anything except nark's reports.'[28]

*Shalamov also describes a 'game' played by prisoners at the Dzhelgala camp and invented by the two informers, Krivitsky and Zaslavsky. They left a piece of bread on a table and hid in the corner. When a starving prisoner came in and tried to seize it, they jumped out and beat him half to death.

And, finally, we reach the masses of ordinary 'political' prisoners, the corpus vile on which the other grades of society exercised their extreme oppressions.

Of them it can be said that in principle they represented every section of the Soviet population. Anyone could become a 'political' prisoner for an indiscreet word, or less. From the beginning of the Kolyma epoch proper, that is in 1937, the area does indeed seem to have been selected by a definite decision as a suitable dumping place for an unusually high proportion of lives regarded as particularly expendable—starting with the Trotskyites and so forth of the *Yezhovshchina*.

Intellectuals abounded. In the ordinary *samizdat* it is common to read in passing that Professor A. A. Mikheev, a botanist, was beaten to death by a guard at Kolyma; that a prominent surgeon was shot for failing to fulfil his norm in the gold mines; that a Polish professor was killed by a blow in the kidneys with a rifle butt; that V. V. Knyazev, a poet admired by Lenin, perished at Magadan (but whose precise date of death, even though he has now been rehabilitated, has not been discoverable even by the Soviet authorities, who give it as '10 November 1937 or, according to other information, March 1938').[11] All camp reminiscences proper teem with descriptions of former academics, administrators, Party officials, scientists, facing pain and humiliation, death by violence and death by exhaustion.

A typical account runs:

My brigade was made up exclusively of former members of the intelligentsia. One of them was Isaac Brevda, a former professor at the Military Medical Academy and an expert in plastic surgery. He was a little, weak and hounded man who had been accused of terrorism, although he started with fright at the very mention of the word. Another man, Vladimir Steklov, was the son of the well-known Bolshevik Yury Steklov-Nakhamkes, one of the veterans of the revolution and former editor of *Izvestia*, who too was jailed in an isolator, either in Syzran or Yaroslavl, for joining the forces of the anti-Stalin opposition. Still another, Nekrasov, a professor of meteorology and an old man, had been sentenced for espionage, although he could not understand what it was he had done to make him a spy. Then there was a former member of the Communist Party and director of some trust, by the name of Ginzburg. There were also engineers, teachers, doctors, and artists. All of them had been seized during the wave of political reprisals launched by the head of the NKVD, Yezhov, and all reached the Kolyma in a condition unfit not only for work, but for living.[23]

One intellectual effort in Kolyma itself is worth recording.

In the hospital at Kilometre 23, a group of nurses and intellectual prisoners, in a unique effort, made an attempt to collect systematic factual evidence of events in Kolyma. They hoped that they might be able to pass it on to posterity, not expecting ever to publish it in their own lifetimes. They were all former members of the Communist Party, and they kept their writing rigorously factual with no commentary at all. They were betrayed by a woman doctor. The alleged ringleader, an old man who had been an agronomist, was shot, and the others got ten years more, for treason, although they had done nothing but draw up a chronicle of the things that happened every day with the knowledge and consent of the government.[13]

Communists who had not adapted themselves to the new Stalinist style of falsification were, of course, common. A typical tale:

I belonged to a political study circle. One day our theme was the October Uprising in Moscow. I had been a soldier under Muralov, one of his artillerymen, and I was wounded twice in the October fighting. I commanded my battery personally against the Junkers at the Nikitsky Gate. In the middle of the lecture the professor asks me:

'Who commanded the Soviet troops in Moscow at the time of the insurrection?'

I answer: 'Muralov, Nikolay Ivanovich Muralov.' I knew him well personally. What else could I say? Eh?

'But that's a provocational answer, Gavril Alexeyevich! You know well that Muralov has been declared an enemy of the people.'

'Well yes, but what do you want me to say? It wasn't in a political study circle that I learnt about the October Revolution.'

They arrested me the same night.[28]

There were representatives of older political trends. Both Lipper and Ginzburg report Social-Revolutionaries, members of the party which had won the majority in the Constituent Assembly, now mostly old women, and we have a very full account by one of these, Ekaterina Olitskaya, who survived her sentence to die in 'free exile' in the area in 1947.[22] Even those who had adjusted to the Soviet regime were of course arrested, as were their children, even if totally non-political. These women, who had often served in Tsarist prisons, were notably educated and intelligent, particularly as compared with the young Communist intake—that is until crushed by the Kolyma system and news of the death of their husbands and sons.

Then there were the Christians. These religious prisoners were the firmest and most unbreakable. They included sects which had been persecuted under Tsardom. Among the women there were nuns. Their convents had, indeed, been destroyed thirty years previously, but they still regarded themselves as bound by their vows.

Elinor Lipper describes how

On all Sundays and church holy days they would go to the lockup. Neither persuasion, threats, mockery nor physical punishment could force them to work on the Lord's Days.

They ate their slender punishment rations and sang their songs. They were beaten. Their skirts were tied over their heads, and sometimes they were tied together by the hair. It did not help. On the following Sunday they allowed themselves to be pushed into the lockup as patiently, submissively, and unflinchingly as ever.[13]

The rigour of the sects' beliefs had already involved them in persecution from Tsardom, which now continued. With some, their religion forbade them even to give their names to Anti-Christ. One woman would never answer roll call with her name. Others used to call out for her, but if there was no friend present she was simply sent to the lockup without food for the night.

Other sects had rules against official documents. In fact, absence of papers had often been the cause of their arrest and conviction. For this fairly minor offence they got only five years. Unfortunately when they were taken for discharge, they refused to accept their discharge papers and were tried and sentenced again.

During the war a number of church dignitaries who had survived were released and restored to office under Stalin's then policy of broadening his support. This did not apply to the rank and file of those sentenced for religious reasons, who remained.

Muslim prisoners from Central Asia and the Caucasus presented a different picture:

Brought from the subtropical climate of their homelands to the coldest regions in the world, they died like flies. All their vital forces were numbed as soon as they went out into the terrible cold. They did not try to defend themselves. They let themselves be driven out to the gold mines. . . . They stood motionless, their arms crossed, their bowed heads hunched between their shoulders, waiting for the end. They made no response at all to orders and curses. Blows were useless—it was as hopeless as asking tin soldiers to bestir themselves.

The decent guards, who realized that these people could not be made to work because in this cold they simply stopped functioning, used their rifle butts to drive the prisoners around and around in a circle, not out of cruelty, but out of pity, because they simply could not look on while the men stood numbed until they fell over like so many dolls. 'Another frozen to death,' the prisoners would note. 'Thermo-shock,' the doctor would record.

When one of them entered the hospital, it was certain that he would leave it feet first. While their Russian comrades fought for life to the last breath, they waited submissively for death. This fatalism, this utter capitulation to the thought of death, made saving them impossible, although Russians with similar cases would overcome the disease. While the Russians patients swallowed their pills with a childlike faith in their curative powers, the Central Asians took the medicine with sceptical indifference, convinced that it would not help at all.

Their traditions forbade them to undress in the presence of a woman, even a nurse. It was a battle every time to give them an injection or an enema. On the other hand, while we had to insist on the Russian patients' washing, these Asiatics were extremely careful about personal cleanliness to the last minute of their lives.

Many died of tuberculosis, many of intestinal diseases, many of pellagra. But the real sickness was the cold, the sunlessness, and the actual imprisonment. These people, many of whom had been nomads, could not endure confinement.[13]

In addition to the more or less permanent intake of intellectuals, and people of non-Communist convictions, the camp population received a variety of additions reflecting the political circumstances. It is even the case that in 1939 a whole category, though a small one, was released from Kolyma altogether. As a result of the Nazi-Soviet Pact, the last voyage of that year saw the shipping out of

German Communists due to be handed over to the Gestapo—among the 570 transferred from NKVD to Gestapo custody at the frontier bridge at Brest-Litovsk that winter.

The same year saw the arrival of the first Poles from Soviet-occupied territory. Many more were to come in 1940. Remarkably few Poles, in fact, seem to have survived to recount their experiences though, unlike their fellow prisoners, those who did survive were released under the Polish-Soviet Treaty of 1941: and various accounts from them are available.

The Poles suffered the disadvantage that they were heavily discriminated against when it came to the 'function' jobs of the camps—which alone gave reasonable chances of surviving. On the other hand, as one of them put it, 'The tremendous difference between us and our fellow convicts was very clear to me here. In spite of everything the Poles waited with hope in their hearts; hope of something, belief in something, and this something was the survival and final liberation, if not of themselves, of the nation and of Poland. Our fellow prisoners hoped for nothing and had faith in nothing.'[2]

Poles and Western Ukrainians were mainly kept in separate camps of poor reputation in the Western Mining Administration. In 1941, at first the Treaty was kept from them: 'While at this forest work, I learned, entirely by chance, about the Polish-Soviet Pact and the "amnesty" affecting all Polish prisoners. I saw the commandant to ask him about this. By way of reply, I was severely punished, having to stand for twenty-four hours in the open, without food.'[2]

However, in late September 1941 the Poles began to be released.

The outbreak of war led in the other direction to the arrival of many Soviet Germans, against whom special discrimination was practised.

At Elgen a special 'German barrack' was set up.

In it were concentrated Germans from Germany and from the Volga Republic, from Siberian and Caucasian villages, Jews from Germany, Austrians, Russians, Hungarians, Finns and Latvians—all 'enemy aliens' in other words, although almost every one of them was a Soviet citizen. They too were employed for heavy 'general' tasks and were the first to be routed out of their beds for nocturnal shock-troop work: otherwise their fate was the same as that of the other prisoners. Only occasionally were they isolated completely in specially remote camps under reinforced guard. Although the idea of this barrack was that Russians, even though prisoners, should not be forced to live with Germans (for all that they were mainly long-since-Russified Volga Germans), the Russian prisoners had a disconcerting habit of wanting to move into this barrack because it was relatively clean, quiet and disciplined, and there was less stealing and swearing in it.[13]

German prisoners of war were comparatively rare in Kolyma, but a few eventually returned to West Germany, where accounts by them, or based on their evidence, were published in the press in the early 1950s.[19, 20] There were a certain number of Japanese P.O.W.s. They were kept in separate camps and only had to work eight hours a day. They usually were employed on road maintenance, but are also noted working in Nagayevo harbour.

The 1943–4 deportation of whole tribes from the Caucasus accused of collaborating with the Germans led to hundreds of them being sent to Kolyma. An account in the Khrushchevite press tells that some of these were sent to a new site, and ordered to clear the ground, to cut timber and construct barracks and watchtowers, an inevitable and integral part of the camp. The Caucasians, not the first to be ordered to perform this work, were certainly the first to refuse to do it. Autumn was fast approaching and the Caucasians, already suffering from the cold, would certainly die if no shelter were provided for them. A team of veteran convicts was despatched to impress upon the recalcitrant Caucasians that their ill-considered gesture of protest would certainly be their death warrant, and, as an additional persuasion, proceeded to set the example of working at the necessary buildings.

The example proved fruitless: the unhappy tribe persisted in crouching about the only tent where their chief lay dying. They wept and they prayed, but they would not budge an inch. The camp commandant was in despair: he had no mandate to cause the death of these men, who were, in any case, in sufficiently large numbers to cause official enquiries into their fate. He therefore asked another team leader to approach their chief, whom he supposed to be some kind of religious leader, to try to persuade him to order his people to work at their own salvation. But when he approached the chief's tent, the despairing cries of the Caucasians told him that the old man had died. All was not lost, however, for, after the chief's funeral which was performed in accordance with strict religious observance, the Caucasians signified their willingness to perform the tasks required of them. They were asked if their chief, in his capacity of religious leader, had left some dying message that they should begin work. The Caucasians replied: 'He was no religious leader, he was the secretary of our District Party Committee.'[29]

In 1944 and 1945 there was an influx from the newly liberated areas. The Baltic states in particular provided thousands of new prisoners. One Lithuanian Jewish woman, all of whose family had been murdered by the Germans in 1941, was sentenced to ten years in 1946 for attempting to leave the country.

In 1946 came a new influx, the 'homecomers'—former

Soviet prisoners of war in Germany, virtually all of whom were sentenced as deserters on return, supplemented by large numbers of women and girls whom the Nazis had deported to work in German munitions plants and who were now sentenced for collaboration.

Other foreigners included numbers of Spaniards. When young children, they had been embarked at Bilbao and elsewhere during the Spanish Civil War, as a humanitarian gesture by the Soviet Union, which had undertaken to look after them. Some 5000 are said to have been shipped thus. In the camps, in the late forties and early fifties, they were young men and women, who had been sentenced usually for theft or prostitution. They had been brought up in orphanages and on leaving had (like many Russians in the same circumstances) drifted into the criminal world. They could remember very little Spanish. Adult Spanish Republicans are of course also reported, just as in other camp areas. One former Republican Air Force captain remained unarrested until 1948, when he unfortunately put in an application to emigrate to Mexico to join his family and so got a 25-year sentence for espionage.

Prisoners who had been working on secret atomic projects in Central Russia, and had finished their terms, now began to be sent in thousands to Kolyma instead of being released. Here they were treated as 'specially dangerous', simply because of the knowledge they might have picked up.[32]

There were also Koreans, described as liable to stab losers at cards unable to pay up even more promptly than other criminals. One Western prisoner took against them when he saw them slaughtering the camp commandant's St Bernard and boiling up its head in the laundry tub.[31]

In 1953, a very special group of prisoners arrived in Magadan. These were the survivors of the great labour camp rebellion which took place at Noril'sk in May of that year. The organisers had managed to spread it to all the camps of the area, till it involved some 55,000 prisoners. They struck for comparatively mild demands—contact with their families, letters and parcels, regularisation of the ration system and so on. Many attempts were made to trick them, but the strike was eventually put down by force, with over 1000 dead. Executions of 'ringleaders' followed on a mass scale. The rebellion's rank and file were sent for special punishment to Kolyma. On their arrival the women's camp at Magadan was evacuated for them as a transit area and equipped with fresh searchlights, six small watchtowers and an immense thickness of fresh barbed wire. Everything that could be used as a weapon, from stones to nails, was removed. The prisoners were marched up by soldiers in full battle equipment, accompanied by armoured cars.

They had already shown resistance, refusing to disembark till the procurator had arrived and guaranteed fair treatment.

After a month in Magadan they were sent on to the notorious mines of Kholodnaya. An old inmate describes them marching to their trucks, shouting boasts and sneering at the meeker prisoners who had preceded them and some of them even singing Ukrainian nationalist songs.[31]

We may conclude this brief conspectus with a Soviet account (of the Khrushchev period) which shows the traditional 'political' pretexts still as flourishing as ever. Three youths of about seventeen years of age arrived in one of the gold camps. They looked younger than their age, perhaps because they were so thin as to be almost emaciated. They announced their names respectively as Yura, Nikita and Vladlen (short for Vladmir Lenin). It was the latter boy who was the cause of the downfall of his two companions. His father, an old Bolshevik, had been killed in the war, and when going through his possessions afterwards,

Vladlen had found a collection of V. I. Lenin's works. In the very last volume he had found an envelope containing a copy of 'Lenin's Testament'. Vladlen was overcome by a boyish temptation to show this off to his comrades although an old friend of his late father's advised him to keep it hidden. Vladlen, although he knew that the advice was good, could not help showing his find to his friends, the matter was reported to the authorities, and he and his closest associates were arrested on the accusation of terrorism and counter-revolution, and sentenced to fifteen years. So there they all were—three boys, two girls and others of the youthful group dispersed in other prison camps.

The prisoners were sorry for their youth and weakness and hunted for something to give them to eat, and pressed them to take the places nearest the stove. The remark of an old Ukrainian appeared a fitting comment: 'They have not enough men to send us now, so they have to send children.'[29]

We shall be dealing with the living—and dying—conditions facing this wide variety of prisoners in a later chapter. Meanwhile, though, it will be appropriate to note a certain hierarchy of suffering. It was often a matter of chance if a prisoner was sent to a 'bad' camp or not; and chance almost always played a part in survival. But there were also institutionalised differences in the prisoners' lot.

Among politicals there was a small proportion in Kolyma who had been sentenced under Article 58(x), for anti-Soviet agitation merely and not terrorism or espionage. Unlike all other politicals, these were not absolutely excluded from the possibility of privileges otherwise only granted to *urkas*, and they were not, or not automatically, given the worst and most back-breaking jobs.

At the other extreme came the lowest and most oppressed category of all—those sentenced not merely for Counter-Revolutionary Activity (KRD), but for Counter-

Revolutionary *Trotskyite* Activity (KRTD). These were not, of course, Trotskyites in any sense: all genuine Trotskyites—and there were very few of these—had been shot by 1937. The expression now meant only that the victim had for some reason, or by chance, incurred the special hatred of one or other official involved, and was thus subject to the worst accusation available. Anyone who had the fatal letter T (Trotskyite) on his dossier was the subject of 'special instructions' which ran: 'During detention forbid all use of post and telegraph. Use only for the hardest labour, report on the conduct of the accused once every three months.' This was a 'passport to death'.

Shalamov describes a prisoner who managed to save his life by getting a typist to drop the T from KRTD when re-copying his dossier for the camp file.

When, after about 1943, the new category came in of *katorzhnik*, serving *katorga* or hard penal servitude (usually with a 20 to 25 year sentence), these were the worst treated of all. It was commoner in Kolyma than in the other main camp areas. They could not in any circumstances be used except for hard physical labour. They were transported in chains. 'They lived in barracks on bare boards in three tiers, without straw mattresses or blankets, so that they never dared to take off any of their wet work clothes. They were granted a blanket only after three years of good conduct. Their camps were totally isolated from all other prison camps. All contact with the outside world, all correspondence was forbidden to them.'[13] They did not survive.

In *katorga*, and even in ordinary camps, the prisoners lived far worse than a final group of living beings to whom we have not yet referred—the animals. The dogs—wolfhounds—were a constant presence in Kolyma. They accompanied all marches and were trained on command to attack people in prison clothes. There are many tales of prisoners savaged, and sometimes killed. Their rations were extremely good, better than that of the guards let alone the prisoners.

Not only the dogs but also the horses enjoyed better conditions than the prisoners. Lipper tells a story, much spoken of in the camps, of a man who in 1944 at the Burkhala camp asked to be regraded as a horse. When he explained to the commandant that he would then get one day off in every ten, and be assigned work according to his strength and have his own stable and blanket, the commandant first gave him ten days in the cells, but after thinking it over, issued him with a new jacket and a month's highest ration.[13]

It is worth telling even this single example of good humour. The extreme rarity of the faintest sign of humanity in the system is, however, its most striking characteristic.

Speaking specifically from experience of Kolyma, a prisoner sums up the effects of the whole system, on all its inmates, good or bad,

A Soviet camp is an incubator for all the vilest human instincts. Its name, 'corrective labour camp', is a mockery. The only things that are corrected in such camps are the methods of petty occasional criminals, who leave the camp trained professional thugs. Not only does the camp provide no educational work; it gives the criminals the finest opportunities to practise their profession. The thief steals, the speculator speculates, the prostitute sells herself. Not only that. The normal person is perverted, the honest man becomes a hypocrite, the brave man a coward, and all have their spirits and bodies broken.[13]

CHAPTER FIVE

GOLD UNDER ICE:
THE KOLYMA ECONOMY

GEOGRAPHICALLY and organisationally, the exploitation of
Kolyma was centred on Magadan (and nearby Nagayevo).
We have seen how the original buildings and roads were
constructed from scratch by the first wave of prisoners. In
1936 the town of Magadan was still unimpressive. The only
brick buildings were the post office, the automobile-repair
plant and the power station. Everything else was of wood,
and mostly mere logs at that. The main road, which went
on to become the Kolyma Highway leading out for 400
miles to Seimchan, was paved; but other streets were not,
and were impassable after rain. There were few street lights.
But though three-quarters of the population were prisoners,
robberies were rare, since the administration had kept in
the town, apart from politics, only the less violent of the
privileged criminal class—'embezzlers, speculators, chisel-
ers, bigamists, the most flagrant violators of the alimony
laws and others composing the cream of Kolyma society'.[23]
Moreover, since the penalty for a prisoner found com-
mitting some offence like theft or making love was to be
shipped at once to the goldfields, there were not many
transgressions.

By the mid-forties Magadan had become a handsome
little city, of 70,000 inhabitants, with electrical workshops,

a small shipbuilding works (at Nagayevo), a 'House of Culture' containing a cinema, a stage, a ballroom and a library (cultural standards were higher, owing to the presence of talented prisoners, than in Vladivostok). The key points in the town, however, were the vast offices of Dalstroy and the NKVD and the huge transit camp which provided the labour for the mines up-country as replacement became necessary—that is, continually.

The main gold deposits were to be found in the upper, hilly stretch of the Kolyma, south and west of Seimchan. The first great expeditions of 1932–3 worked the old mines centred on the one hand on the area where the Magadan–Seimchan road reaches the river, which included the original site of Boriskin, together with Srednikan and others; and on the other the area further up the river around Yagodnoye, including such sites as Khatenakh and At-Uryakh. These became the Southern and Northern Administrations respectively. By 1938, the Northern Administration was running eight main mines, employing among them over 50,000 prisoners. The total in all the Kolyma mines was now about 150,000.

Expansion was continual. By 1938 a new Western Administration had come into existence, and by 1940 South-Western, North-Western, Chai-Urya and Tyenkino-Detrinsk Administrations were operating. (The Western seems to have covered the area over the passes from Berelyakh, and the North-Western the further extension into the Indigirka valley around Oymyakon. The South-Western was in fact situated in the easterly direction. The Chai-Urya lay in the more inaccessible areas east of the Kulu, while the Tyenkino-Detrinsk was in even more difficult country south-west of the most southerly bend of the Kolyma.)

In 1940, these 7 administrations ran no less than 66 mines. The extension by opening up new areas had been matched by further finds in the old areas—so that the Northern Administration, for example, had 12 main mines in 1940. The numbers of prisoners in the gold camps had risen to over 400,000.

Expansion continued. A first attempt to open up the Pestraya Dresva area was made in the summer of 1940. Several thousand prisoners and about 800 free citizens were embarked. The winter clothes were inaccessible at the bottom of the hold when the cold weather set in, and there was much frostbite en route. They were landed, in conditions somewhat resembling the first 'assault' on Magadan in 1932, but weather and sea conditions made it impossible to build the base harbour. After thousands of deaths, the survivors had to be re-embarked and the project was abandoned.

In the spring of 1941 the remnant of the expedition was unloaded in the port of Magadan: two hundred free men and a hundred and fifty prisoners. In the prison hospital at Magadan, where I was working as a nurse at this time, these hundred and fifty were laid side by side on cots in three barracks. They were hollow-eyed relics of humanity, but they kept silent about the horrors they had endured; only those in the delirium of pneumonia screamed out their memories. The frightful stench of rotting human flesh filled the barracks.

The morning after their arrival the surgeon came with his assistants and his instruments and went down the line. With the aid of the nurses the sick were sat up and their arms stretched out at right angles to their chests, palms down. Then the surgeon cut off the frozen, suppurating fingers. Twenty-five cots along one wall, twenty-five cots along the opposite wall. The bits of flesh in the kidney-shaped bowl piled up. After the fingers came the toes.

Those were the light cases. Others were left with stumps of arms and legs. A good many survived the pneumonia, and when they awoke for the first time after long days of fever and coma they looked for their limbs, but the limbs were gone. For many, medical care came too late and they died of blood poisoning. Unknown Soviet heroes. No newspapers mention them. There is only a number on their nameless graves.[13]

A later and better-prepared attempt finally opened up the area, and by 1949 20,000 prisoners were working in four mines, based in Omsuchkan.

There was continuous prospecting and an extension of mining in all likely areas. The fields on the lower Yana, on the Arctic Ocean, were developed. In addition to the gold camps whose existence we know of, there must have been a fair number of others, on the Yana and elsewhere, which have not been registered in records reaching the West. It seems probable that eventually some half a million prisoners were in the mines—and this, of course, is not to include prisoners working at other projects, of which we shall treat later in this chapter.

The gold of Kolyma is, in one way, specially suited to manual labour. That is, much of it lies in surface deposits not more than a few metres down into the soil, even though usually within the permafrost, meaning work that was both hard and cold. Veins were of course also discovered, and proper mines opened to develop them; and these became increasingly important as the more accessible deposits became exhausted. But the expression 'mine' used of the gold camps covered every sort of excavation.

For the surface mining preliminary work was often done before the 100-day official season—mainly the removal of the deep layers of peat which make the top level in most of Kolyma. In some areas detachments then went out to sift the upper surface. An account in the Soviet press tells of how two men had to start a bonfire. This had to be done without matches, by the ancient method of striking sparks with flints. Another man had to fetch water from the frozen river and melt it. The deeply frozen ground next had to be softened, then excavated and the sand passed through sieves in search for gold.[29]

Elsewhere the surface gold was more concentrated, and whole teams worked a site intensively. A Pole describes the methods: 'The work on the surface consisted of digging earth, often mixed with gravel. We dug with crowbars, picks and shovels, and in winter when the ground was frozen, with gouges. . . . The daily norm was 125 barrows of earth dug, which had then to be pushed to a distance of from 300 to 400 metres.'[2]

These excavations merged insensibly into true surface-mining:

We were set to work to open up the mine, which was later named for the famous aviator, Vodopyanov. The work was back-breaking. We had to dig holes in the frozen earth with picks in order to plant dynamite for blasting. Often, before getting to solid soil, there was peat to be removed— sometimes as deep as five feet. For this work we only had the simplest tools—shovels and pickaxes—and in winter, sleds to which we harnessed ourselves. Later, when the work of development had progressed further, machines began to be brought in. . . .[10]

Finally, and increasingly, there were genuine under-ground mines. One prisoner describes how 'Below the surface these mines were 120–150 feet deep, and ac-cidents . . . were frequent, as many as five or six a day. The underground corridors were narrow and the ceilings not propped. The unfortunate victims of accidents were hauled to the surface, their hands cut off in proof of death (to be shown to the authorities) and the bodies then thrust below the brushwood.'[2]

Another tells us that, 'In the underground mines machine drills and explosive drills and explosive cartridges filled with ammonal are used. The pace of work is so furious that the use of explosives occasions frequent accidents and prisoners are crippled or killed. There are also many tales of despairing workers who blow themselves up.'[13]

In winter,

Technically, the work proceeded as follows: in the mine drifts the workers bored and blasted the sands, which were then raked away and heaped into a single pile. The ends of steamhoses connected to boilers standing outside the barrack were then driven into the pile. The steam was released and the sands were thawed out somewhat. Then they were carried in wheelbarrows to the panning unit. Carloads of ice were also thawed out by steamhoses, and the sands were washed with the water thus obtained. After the washing, the water flowed off into a deep pool,where it was allowed to settle and later used again.

From the technical point of view, winter panning under such conditions bordered on insanity, since, in the first place, the sands were never thawed out properly, and, second, the apparatus was extremely inadequate. Geological analysis established that close to three-fourths of the gold was carried off instead of being retained in the apparatus. However, the plan for gold production fixed for Dalstroy remained unfulfilled, and Moscow demanded gold. According to computations by economists, each gram of gold obtained during winter washing cost approximately four times the number of working hours it required in summer. Despite these facts, panning continued.[23]

A free citizen was told that 'Each worker must work eight cubic metres of rock per day. If he does not do this, his bread ration is reduced. If he exceeds the norm, his ration is increased. As only a few are capable of achieving the output required in the time, the majority work considerably more than the officially laid down working day.'[33]

A prisoner was able to recall the labour imposed by Tsardom, under Nicholas I, on the Decembrist rebels forced to work in the Nerchinsk goldfield: 'I told him, from the "Tales of Maria Volkonskaya", the rigorous treatment that they had inflicted on the Decembrists: each of them had to hew 50 kilograms. . . .

' "And what's our norm, Vasily Petrovich?" Fedyakhin asked.

'I calculated: "About a ton and a half!"

' "You see, Vasily Petrovich, the norms have progressed." '[28]

The gold was put into leather bags containing 20 kilograms of dust and screwed into special wooden crates and sent under heavy guard to Magadan. In the mid-thirties, it was flown directly to Moscow to a special NKVD gold refinery. Later, when production increased, we are told that the gold was sent in a special destroyer to Vladivostok, on the first leg of its journey to Moscow.

Gold production in the late thirties seems to have reached about 300 tons a year, and after the war to have gone up to from 400 to 500 tons a year (getting on for a third of world production). As we have seen, one estimate is that every ton of Kolyma gold cost about a thousand human lives.

Though gold remained the staple product of the whole Dalstroy–Kolyma enterprise, there were other products —for example, the lead mines on the Chukhotsk peninsula. These were operated without safety measures (at least in 1940–1) and all prisoners eventually died of lead poisoning. This applied, for example, to 3000 Poles sent there in August 1940, about whom no action had to be taken when the amnesty for Polish citizens came into force at the end of the following year, since none of them was left alive.[2]

With the American entry into the war later in 1941, gold became less immediately necessary to the Soviet rulers on account of the Lend-Lease system. The plan for gold production was slightly curtailed. Lead and tin mining on the other hand was intensified (and a new effort went into road-building). Other mining included the great coal mines of Arkagala, to the north-west. These eventually supplied the entire region. In the same area, uranium was eventually discovered. And at the beginning of 1952, it was decided to build a vast nuclear plant at a spot known as 754 (its distance in kilometres from Magadan)—otherwise as D-2. It was to be operated by free workers, but built by prisoners. Some ten thousand were assembled. There was the usual trouble with inefficient planning, resulting in the warping of floors and inefficient and unsafe use of labour. Security was intense, and we only have one brief account from a foreigner who was accidentally posted there for a few days.[31]

Road construction and maintenance remained a continual and heavy burden on resources and on labour, with its own Administration (originally sited at Yagodnoye), ranking with and evidently employing as many labourers as a mining administration. —And the roads were also regular customers for a supply of logs from the lumber teams. These were of course needed for other purposes too, such as camp construction. And logging remained, as elsewhere in the Soviet North, a major employment.

In 1941 ten thousand of the strongest prisoners were transferred from the Northern Administration alone to the Road-Building Administration, to build the road to the Indigirka River and beyond. This road, known as Kolyma *Trassa*—the Kolyma Trace, still exists. It is in part roughly metalled and in part merely a mud track across the taiga. A Russian who used it in 1965 says that there were still many camps in operation across the whole stretch, by now extended to Irkutsk.

As with the coal of Arkagala, and the wood of the forests, it was Dalstroy's policy to be self-sufficient in every respect. One essential product alone could not be raised in Kolyma—wheat. ('Of course', a free vi˙ or noted, 'other foodstuffs are imported into the territory for officials, and receptions at, for example, Nikishov's . . . were notable for their lavishness.')[33]

But, except as regards bread, the staple foodstuffs were produced locally. There were large 'State Farms', entirely staffed by women prisoners, · at Dukcha, Susuman and elsewhere. Their main product was cabbage. The coarse outer leaves were used for prisoners in a brew called 'khaki soup' because of its greenish-brown colour. The cabbage heads were sent to free citizens. Some potatoes were also planted, although in much smaller quantities, and solely for the free population. In addition, turnips were grown, together with oats which did not ripen but were used as cattle fodder.[13]

A Polish woman describes one of the farming camps:

The site of the camp in Talon is very beautiful. Meadow-land, ringed in by vast forests, one side bounded by a chain of mountains, the other by a wide, slow-flowing river. The air fresh and keen. Beyond the forest, swamp. The tilled land produces potatoes, turnips, cabbage, low-growing oats. Here order was kept in the barracks and the 'politicals', incredibly, were better thought of than the apaches and other criminals. This is the only time I experienced this. The barracks are roomy and light, with pallet-beds. Between the beds are empty packing-cases for lockers and some chairs. . . .

We worked long shifts in the fields, cutting and loading sackfuls of cabbage. With my terrible discharging sores, it was very difficult for me to pack, sew up and load the enormous sacks. Hands and arms were covered with blood; the cold entered all my open wounds. The apache women lit great fires in the fields, but they would not let us other women near. . . .

My legs and hands now became so full of pus that I was put to work with old Jaga, plaiting straw slippers. Four of us worked in a tiny log hut, with a stove in the middle, minute windows, a wooden wheel, and straw stuffed between the logs in an attempt to keep out the bitter wind. Jaga was very old. All day long she sang and told tales; old tales of the time of the Tsars, full of magicians, bishops, enchanted wolves, sunsets and moonrise, sleigh rides and Easter joy. . . . Only the very infirm were allowed to do this work. Among us were a former colonel (Tsarist) whose spine had been permanently injured during interrogation, a former noble who had been educated in Warsaw, a former engineer (Soviet), blinded in a gold mine, old Jaga, and myself, a former human being and a Pole.[2]

More important still, and constituting an export as well as a useful local foodstuff, was fishing. On the Okhotsk Sea, there were five large fishing camps, with both men and women prisoners: at Nagayevo, Ola, Balagannoye, Yana and Arman. And similar camps existed on the Arctic Ocean at Ambarchik and on the Bear Islands. Herring and various types of salmon were the main product, salt herring being a normal part of the prisoners' diet.

Working conditions in the fishery camps were different from those of the gold and other camps, in the nature of the job. Balagannoye is described as one of the most tolerable camps of Kolyma. It was 'divided into two parts by a high wooden palisade and by barbed wire; one part is for women, the other for the men prisoners who are crippled, too weak, or too ill to work in the gold mines, and who therefore are employed as porters and drivers, woodsmen, and craftsmen.'[13]

At Arman, the women fish-packers noted that

Our clothes, our blankets, even the planks we slept on, were always streaming and full of salt. Our boots, if we took them off at night, were shapeless and sticky like gloves washed on the hands when we came to put them on again next morning. Our clothes came off only once a week, when we went to the bath-house. . . .

Two women working together are supposed to pack and salt away 6600 salmon in one day. In itself the effort of reaching down to the bottom of the great kegs is enough to exhaust the strength of a healthy woman properly fed. The pain in our arms and shoulders was excruciating. We felt as if we were being flayed by the salt, the water and the movements we had to make. We worked a shift of twelve hours inside refrigerators. Scales lay about our feet in drifts. . . . Among the barrels, a few couples were always lying in hurried, sodden and animal embrace. After some days I was moved from the kegs to the gutting-alleys. I forget exactly how many I was expected to gut a day. I think it was 1700. The doctor was a kind woman, herself serving a sentence of twenty-five years. She spoke French, but in secret only. It was to her that I owed the change of work.[2]

This prisoner adds (like her fellow convict at Balagannoye) that nevertheless,

Apart from the actual nature of the work (which was the most exhausting I experienced anywhere) this was not the worst camp one could find. . . .

The food, too, was good by comparison. Soup made of fish heads in the morning, kasha with pieces of fish at noon and salmon fried in seal fat for our dinner. The star workers got a kilo of bread, but few of us ever passed 50 per cent of the norm and got only 500 grams of bread and small portions of the other foods. Those lower than 50 per cent got only 300 grams of bread, with soup.[2]

In addition to the mining of non-precious metals and of coal, the production of logs and of food, there was a whole range of subsidiary enterprises, such as sewing shops, a glass factory, power stations, brick-works, an electro-engineering plant at Atka, which manufactured electric motors; a metallurgical plant at Orotukan, where there were iron deposits; and so forth.

Gold, however, remained the great central focus of the economy of Kolyma, with most of its other operations ancillary to that main thrust. This remained true in spite of the fact that the road-builders and fish-packers, the menial workers of Magadan and the turnip growers of Ola, constituted a fair proportion of the total labour force—even though, as far as possible (and it was not always possible), women and 'goners' were used. Perhaps a third of Kolyma's prisoners at any given time were, in one capacity or another, not at the gold face. The miners nevertheless, in their hundreds of thousands, were the real cannon fodder of the enterprise.

Of course, it is plain that (as even works published in the USSR, such as that of General Gorbatov, have stressed) the way the prisoners were used, the total disregard of human resources, was insanely wasteful. That is, indeed, to assume, and to assume wrongly, that the economic motive predominated, and that the aim of destroying the prisoners was not in itself at least equally compelling for the Stalinist administration.

But even in its purely economic attitudes, the regime had a built-in tendency to enormous errors and inefficiencies. For example, much winter work was done in prospecting, with prisoners being sent to drive shafts deep into the permafrost, particularly harsh and dangerous work. Five hundred prisoners were sent out for this in March 1938, at Zarosshy Spring. Half of them died. The area proved unproductive and the shafts were abandoned. In March 1940, prisoners were sent to exactly the same area for the same work, with the same results.[32]

The mere utilisation of machinery was impossible to organise effectively under the pressures of the time. There are many stories of machines wrecked because the foremen could not provide proper maintenance and the prisoners were forced to use them beyond their capacity.

Even more extraordinary stories are told of losses due to organizational inefficiency. In 1939 one prisoner

had a talk with the norm-setter of the mine's Planning

Section—a free employee. He told me that the productivity of labour in the pits was approximately three-fourths of that of the preceding year, and only one-fourth of that of 1937. The situation was partly corrected by the presence of three excavators which managed to do some of the work despite the difficulties of operating in perpetually frozen soil. I asked how the large 'Marion' excavator of American origin, imported a year earlier, was functioning. He thought for a while.

'Marion, Marion . . . I remember we had one by that name. But where is it? Last year I heard that it was working poorly and very little: some mistakes had been made in assembling it, then there was some breakage, and it stopped working altogether. I have no idea where it is now, though I know all our sections . . . sections . . .'

'I remember it was said last year that it was paid for in gold, something like $20,000, apart from transport costs,' I remarked. . . .

Two days later I saw him again. He came to where I worked and sat down on the embankment.

'You've started something now. There is quite a mess. I ran through every mine looking for the excavator, and then reported to the director that it had disappeared. He raised everyone to their feet and now we are all running about searching for it . . . '

I burst out laughing. The supposition that a huge excavator could disappear without a trace from a relatively small gold field seemed extremely amusing. The fact that picks and shovels, wheelbarrows and wagons were lost by the hundreds in the blasting operations, to the complete indifference of everyone, that the rails of the mechanical tracks rusted through and vanished under piles of rock and ore, that building timber was burned in the ovens and boilers—all this was perfectly normal and taken for granted in every Soviet enterprise. But an excavator! A huge, expensive imported machine! This was too much even for the camp administration. No one could have stolen it, especially since, when it was last seen, it was inactive, broken by unskilled mechanics. Besides, who would steal an excavator at the gold fields!

Looking at me with chagrin, the norm-setter said:

'Well, what are you laughing at? Do you know what trouble this might mean for me? I was one of three persons who signed the inventory of October the first, certifying the presence of a "Marion" excavator at the mine. And now it is not here. It is true that formally the warehouse-keeper of the 3rd Section is responsible for it, but the trouble is that he was transferred six months ago to the new Western Mining Administration, and the transfer was so hurried that he had no time to explain all his affairs to the new man. And now no one can say who will be answerable.'

I understood all that, knowing the system of complicated book-keeping controls in Soviet institutions, a system which, however, was quite powerless to eliminate the crying inefficiency everywhere. . . .

The puzzle of the excavator's disappearance was cleared up in the fall, and then quite by accident. The geologists found that one of the previous year's dumps was lying on ground with a high gold content, and it was necessary to carry it to a new place, which had already been mined. One of the new excavators was assigned to this work since the earth to be moved was not frozen hard and therefore the excavator could be of use. One day the scoop of the excavator caught against something in the dump and broke; the men began to dig, and found, under a solid layer of earth, the vanished 'Marion', thoroughly rusty and battered. How this huge machine could have been buried under the refuse without anyone seeing it or taking note remained a mystery. In the field records the excavator was written off as iron scrap.[23]

Even more basic to disastrous mismanagement was the Stalinist planning principle under which the slogan 'There are no fortresses a Bolshevik cannot storm' was interpreted in such a way that it became impossible to criticise planning far beyond the capacity of an enterprise without running the risk of arrest for 'counter-revolutionary norm-setting'. All over the USSR crazed or ambitious officials ruined their saner rivals, and imposed in all fields the over-utilization of resources, or even plans which had no more basis than their very grandiosity. Moreover the planning process proper, within which these attitudes took effect, was heavily over-bureaucratized and (especially in Kolyma) lacking in real connection with the problems on the spot. In minor building, for example, as early as 1937:

Under Soviet procedure even such petty construction activities as ours had to be approved in Moscow, by the Ministry, and the latter, lacking any knowledge of the actual local needs, often included in the plan completely unnecessary units and omitted the essential ones. As a result, a mine might be in need of a bakery, but would be required by plan to build a bath-house. Or it might need a bath-house, but the plan would provide money for building breeding kennels for bloodhounds; or else money would be allotted for the construction of a communal dwelling, while the mine director wanted to build a new house for himself, with but a single apartment. Then a series of complicated combinations would begin. In its reports, the mine would show the building of a dining-hall for prisoners, when in fact a dormitory for the guards had been erected. Naturally, the bank knew nothing and issued money for a dining-hall. The bank was not concerned with whether the kennels were needed by the mine: if kennels were ordered, they had to be built! But under Kolyma conditions, when all local power was in the hands of Dalstroy, and the bank's sole repre-sentative was the ever-hungry inspectress Sveshnikova, the bank's actual powers of control were reduced to zero.

However, within the mining administration, the con-struction activities were also controlled by the Building Section, which in effect said to the mine: 'You may break the law, but only with our permission.' And the mine director knew that if our section should report his illegal building work to the bank, the money would be stopped at once, and, if things took a bad turn, he might even end up on the defendant's bench. If, luckily, his mine fulfilled the gold production norm, he could reasonably expect leniency. . . . But if, in addition to everything else, the mine produced less gold than was required of it, then no power on earth could save the mine administration from serious difficulties.[23]

The construction of a 3000-kilowatt electric power station at Taskan ran into the other and equally common trouble of arbitrary and ill-informed orders.

Despite the constant pushing by Pavlov himself, the survey of that area prolonged itself. Pavlov lost patience and made a personal appearance on the spot in the middle of winter, mercilessly berated all the geologists, cast his ruler's eye over the region, pointed out a site for the erection of the powerhouse, and ordered immediate excavations. Within a week about a thousand workers were herded to the spot, and all winter they dug the ground for the foundations of the powerhouse. However, when the snow melted, it turned out that the spot chosen was in the middle of a swamp and there could be no question of building anything there. Everything had to be started anew. Fortunately for the geologists, the head of the prospecting party had succeeded in obtaining from Pavlov a written order for the starting of operations on the spot determined by the eccentric's whim, and therefore no reprisals followed the initial fiasco.[23]

Another construction job of the same period, also in the Taskan area,

was the laying of a single-track suspension railway. By that time the problem of supplying the mines with construction lumber and firewood had become extremely complicated, since all more or less suitable timber had been ruthlessly destroyed within a radius of 30–40 miles. The nearest forests of suitable size were . . . separated from the gold fields by a wide stretch of impassable swamps. The lack of transportation facilities and the general acuteness of the problem made it necessary to find some way out of the difficulty; as a result, it was decided to build a suspension railway on piles dug deeply into the earth. Along this railway, suspended cars were to ply back and forth, carrying lumber to the fields. . . . Its total mileage, to begin with, was to be 25 miles. . . .

Since the Industrial Bank refused to grant any funds for so risky a venture, some simple book-keeping manipulations were indulged in, and the financing was started at the expense of basic production—the expense of costs per gram of gold.

The whole story ended ingloriously. Work went on for about eight months, but when spring arrived it became clear that the implacable swamp would brook no intrusion: all the piles that had been driven into the earth in winter began to settle down and sag in various directions as the ground thawed out. The road laid over them, with here and there the rails already in place, turned into such a bent and twisted line that there could be no question of moving cars with lumber along it. Work was stopped. A part of the construction timber that went into the road was salvaged for fuel, and the rest was abandoned without use. The administration wrote off a loss of about a million and a half rubles.[23]

Similar stories come from all periods and areas of Kolyma. Ten years later, the building of a factory in the Pestraya Dresva region was 'speeded up' by the simple act of the chief NKVD official (evidently General Derevenko) who, on being told that it could not be ready until November, wrote on the file 'the factory must be ready unconditionally not later than May 1.'[31] As a result of the pace, and the lack of equipment, it then took a year longer than the original plan and cost double.

In the same area and period a Czechoslovak engineer prisoner, Venyamin Piscun, reports a vast error almost precisely parallelling the Taskan railway fiasco:

At the Galimyy mines they were working on four levels and drilling new sections, so that the ore output would be trebled. They found that their huge Diamond-T trucks could not cope with the increase. Apart from that they considered it unpatriotic to shell out dollars, or even gold, for tires and spare parts. So they decided that the cheapest way to solve the truck and fuel problem would be to build a funicular transportation system from the top of the mountain and string it four miles down to the factory below. They had the poles, they had the cable-cars. The missing link was the cable. Funicular cables are specially made, and their production requires great skill and experience. At that time the only such plant was in Leningrad. They wrote to Leningrad and were told that, due to the large number of orders on hand, the request could not be filled for five years!

A Party meeting was immediately convened to solve the problem. The hotheads shouted, 'There are no fortresses that we cannot conquer! We shall build the cable with our own hands!' He meant *our* hands, of course. Some older members tried to talk them out of it, but the hotheads had it their own way. I was called in for technical advice, and gave them a categorical NO. But who was I, a convict, a traitor to his motherland. They knew better. So they went ahead, twisting the wires around a wooden device invented by some cabinet-maker. One day it was ready, and thousands of prisoners were marched up the icy slopes of the mountain, lugging the homemade cable on their shoulders. The day came when the first empty cable-car left the top and reached the plant below. Then another, half loaded. Then a third, fully loaded. Everything looked wonderful. They decided to celebrate. They put flags on each pole, they brought a brass band, and then decided that some top officials should go down the mountain by cable to show how safe it was. The officials piled in, the band played, and loud hurrahs went up as the cable-car took off. It had hardly gone a hundred yards when suddenly the cable began to stretch, and as a result the cable-car sagged to the ground. No one was injured, but neither did anybody have the courage to propose another homemade cable. As for the poles, they remained as a reminder of this costly bungle, but because they were not buried in deep enough they now look like sagging crosses in an old cemetery![31]

In fact, the economy was beset by inhuman pressures and functioned with a maximum of friction, as well as of terror, as a result. A typical story, in which these pressures are seen not on the grand scale but as they affected the ordinary mining gang, well conveys the spirit of the times:

A dark hole in the rib of a desolate mountain was the usual entrance to a mine. Digging was made at various levels with some of the prisoners working at the surface and others 2500 or 3000 yards below. The tunnels inside the mines were so narrow that two people could hardly walk side by side, and the height hardly permitted a medium-sized fellow to walk unless bent from the middle. In some places the gallery was so badly excavated that we had to advance on our knees and hands. Until the end of the 1950s when Humphrey's safety lamps were distributed, every prisoner-miner had to provide his own light which was a rusted tin with a wick dipped in some grease. This gave a very poor light; under the drafts it was often snuffed out. The worst situation was when the naked light came in contact with gases emanating from crevasses and other cracks in the mine's walls and caused an explosion. Trunks of trees, which should have been used as pillars of support for the galleries, were sometimes sawed and taken away in the dark by prisoners who used them in the barracks as firewood. Until late in the 1950s prisoners were still working with picks and axes as their only tools, while their legs could hardly move from the heavy chains.

The loading of excavated material was done in three-quarter-ton cars pushed with bare hands to the pit's mouth where other prisoners took over, sorting the rich ore from the waste rock.

For the prisoners who used the primitive lifts for descending into the mines there was a terrible risk, as the cables holding the lifts were old and rusty, and more than once they snapped under the load of the humans they were taking below.

The work in the mines was a nightmare. No precautions were taken to protect the workers against accidents. Eventually the miners got carbide lamps, and a privileged few were given lamps with electric batteries. The officials also began to pump fresh air into the mines, but due to the administrative panic to reach the projected production levels, the air was always filled with heavy dust. As a result, many developed silicosis.

Not a single day would go by without an accident being reported. Either the power supply would fail and prisoners would get stuck halfway, or a cable would snap and the lift would crash. The maimed and badly injured were constantly being hauled off to the camp hospital. Lack of headgear caused more accidents. Miners wore their Russian fur hats instead of helmets, and when large stones and rocks poured down, a man was done for.

The terror of failing to meet the daily quota kept the brigade leaders and the men in a constant state of frenzy. They knew how many three-quarter-ton cable-cars they had to send down daily, and they knew that each cable-car was carefully checked when it arrived. I witnessed a scene when, at the end of our shift, the brigade leader, a man named Gregoryev, questioned the prisoner assigned by the administration to check the output. The man was covered in dirt from head to foot, and his eyes were red from dust.

'How many cable-cars did we send down today?' asked Gregoryev in a hoarse voice.

'Fourteen!'

'Fifteen,' roared Gregoryev. 'Not one less.'

'I'm sorry,' said the checker, 'there were only fourteen.'

'What do you want?' screamed Gregoryev at the top of his voice. 'That my men should go hungry because of a few stones! Put down fifteen on your tally sheet. If you don't I'll kill you right here.'

'I cannot, brother,' cried the other. 'I swear I cannot. . . .'

He never finished his sentence. Gregoryev pulled out a thin-bladed knife and plunged it several times into the man's chest. The man lay dead, and Gregoryev ran away after spitting on the body and hissing:

'For a dog, a dog's death.'[31]

All in all, these conditions reflected one main truth. In the minds of its creators and organisers the conscious purpose of Kolyma, which had originally been the production of gold, with death as an unplanned by-product, had become the production, with at least equal priority, of gold and death.

CHAPTER SIX

LIVING AND DYING CONDITIONS

At Cayenne too it was nasty, but here it
really is very nasty.
A FRENCH PRISONER,
PREVIOUSLY ON DEVIL'S ISLAND. [28]

THE basic principle of Kolyma, that of underfeeding and overworking the prisoner, has already emerged clearly enough in a general way—that system by which the last energies squeezed out of his failing body were used to get the State more gold. We may now consider precisely how the machine worked.

The method by which the Stalin regime extracted further effort from its exhausted victims was, of course, the 'norm system'. The ration was made dependent upon output, so that the urge to survive pressed the prisoner to try to fulfil his set task, and thus achieve the maximum food. At the same time, that best ration was so low as barely to ensure a temporary respite; the work was so hard and long that the struggle was always a losing one; and the norm itself was anyhow set so high that it was very difficult to achieve it regularly. So a precarious balance was reached which—usually—ensured a fair level of gold production while also fulfilling the other main object of Kolyma, the killing off of the prisoners.

The norms varied to some extent through the years (being raised in 1941-2 for example). So did the ration, which also came down during the war, as well as after famine, or near-famine, years like 1947. The general scheme is given, which should put it beyond much dispute, in a Soviet publication of the Khrushchev era:

'The convicts worked a twelve-hour day, and only completion of the norm gave the right to the full 800 grams of bread per day. Non-fulfilment of norms, through whatever cause, automatically entailed a reduction of the bread ration to 500 grams. This was just above the starvation level: any further reduction to 300 grams (as a punitive measure) meant death within a couple of days.'[29]

The slight variations on this to be found in other reports are of no great significance. But we may note that in certain circumstances 'overfulfilment' of the plan might be rewarded with a ration of a full 1000 grams;[18] that an intermediate ration of 700-750 grams is sometimes reported; that women (and men not in the mines) got a lower basic scale of 600 grams for 100 per cent norm, 500 for 70-99 per cent, and 400 for 50-69 per cent; that the penal ration in the lockup was sometimes as low as 200 grams. And, more important, that the 12-hour day was a minimum and in practice it was extended, often to as much as 16 hours.[13]

In addition to the basic bread, other food was provided. One reported supplement, rather better than most, is given as; '3.5 ounces of salted fish; 2.1 ounces of cereals—barley, barley groats, millet, or oats; 0.17 ounce of meal or starch; 0.5 ounce of vegetable oil; 0.34 ounce of sugar; 0.106 ounce of herb tea; 10.5 ounces of brined cabbage leaves.'[13]

It is worth nothing that these rations can readily be compared with a camp system known to Westerners for its horrors—that of the Japanese prisoner-of-war camps on the River Kwai. There the daily ration norm was 700 grams of rice, 600 of vegetables, 100 of meat, 20 of sugar, 20 of salt and 5 of oil. This, notably superior to the Kolyma ration in spite of the latter area's added disadvantage of extreme cold, was also the ration actually delivered and not merely the official figure. Like the Soviet ration, it was, however, greatly deficient in vitamins. It gave a calorie total of about 3400. The Soviet diet in strict-regime camps is, even in 1977, only 2600 calories; punishment diet is still 2100 calories, and prisoners in the strict-punishment cells get 1300. The international standard for a man working 'very actively' for 8 hours a day is 3100 to 3900 calories. The calories deficit alone, to say nothing of vitamins and fats, is thus something like 1000 calories a day at a minimum.

Moreover, as a prisoner notes, 'In evaluating the prison rations it must be kept in mind that these rations are for people who perform the heaviest kind of physical labour twelve, fourteen, and sixteen hours a day in a country which during the eight months of winter has the lowest temperatures of any inhabited country on the face of the earth.'[13]

And it was indeed the heaviest labour. Kolyma is the only area of the whole labour camp system where lumbering is not taken as the hardest and most killing task. For the Kolyma prisoners had to hack not wood but stone, or earth as hard as stone. General I. S. Karpunich-Braven typically describes taking part in 'the removal of "turves" (earth with rock fragments and boulders in it) when the temperature was 50°C. below freezing, transporting them on sledges to which were harnessed four prisoners, beaten as they hauled.'[8]

The prisoners' day thus centred round food and work. A typical one ran on the following lines: Reveille 4 a.m.

Breakfast of gruel plus one-third of the bread ration, or half a herring and bread. 5 a.m., march off to work. Noon, cabbage leaf soup, one-third of the bread ration, groats, or merely gruel and peas. 8 p.m., back to camp, except for those not achieving their norm, who did two hours more. Supper: one-third, of the bread ration and soup, after various camp chores like firewood-collecting had been performed.[18,2]

The fulfilment of the norm was of course made even more difficult by the assignment of part of the output to criminals who had done no real work. In any case

even if the work performed is listed honestly, it is impossible for a person unaccustomed to physical labour to fulfil the quota. He quickly falls into a vicious circle. Since he cannot do his full quota of work, he does not receive the full bread ration; his undernourished body is still less able to meet the demands, and so he gets less and less bread, and in the end is so weakened that only clubbings can force him to drag himself from camp to gold mine. Once he reaches the shaft he is too weak to hold the wheelbarrow, let alone to run the drill; he is too weak to defend himself when a criminal punches him in the face and takes away his day's ration of bread.[13]

The margin was so narrow that every crumb was watched. A woman prisoner gives the atmosphere:

The bread is distributed by a grey-haired old invalid with sharp eyes, a sharp tongue, a thin sharp nose, and thin sharp fingers. In front of her lies a book like the commander of the guard's book, listing the names of all the prisoners by brigades. You give her your name and she begins thumbing through the pages while seventy women wait. She pushes back her glasses, stares at you to make sure you really are the person you claim to be, sets her glasses back on her nose, and hands you the ready-cut seven ounces of bread. It is a middle section, of course; not everybody can have an end of bread. Ends are for her special friends; she cannot befriend everyone. It is impossible to explain to someone who has not been in camp or prison what the end of a loaf of bread means. The end is crisper, it looks more attractive and it seems to be heavier. But more than that, an end mysteriously fills you more than the middle section of the bread, although it too weighs only seven ounces (200 grams). A middle section is a stab wound to the heart; it is a confirmation from Providence that you are abandoned for good and all. It is the beginning of a day in which everything will surely go wrong. And you almost always get a middle section.

Not only on account of the ends is the distributor of bread one of the most hated women in camp. She also has the right to allow for 3 grams of crumbs and moisture for each 200 grams of bread, so that in reality she need give out only 197 grams. What happens to all the crumbs and to the moisture, which is not lost at all, since it is well known that she covers the loaves at night with damp cloths in order to replace whatever moisture may have evaporated? Those extra 3 grams go into her own stomach, or she makes gifts of bread to her bosom friends. It's easy to see how she has filled out since she has held this post. The worst-hated people in camp are the well-fed.[13]

Naturally this system left no allowance for error. Equally naturally, in Soviet conditions, error—or the unforeseen—came often.

This might happen on an individual basis, as when General Gorbatov tells of inedible bread.

Unfortunately the bread he had brought turned out to be sodden and inedible. We were indignant and pressed him to take it back and show it to someone in authority. The man took me aside, explained the situation at the camp, and said: . . .'You're an Article 58 man. If you protest they might take it as insubordination and incitement. That would cost you another five years or ten. I can see for myself the bread's unusable, but that's all you'll get this time so you'll just have to wait a week anyhow whether you like it or not. Why don't you keep it—that would be better—instead of making me take it back. It would be dangerous for me—I'm in the same boat as you.'[5]

Any large-scale dislocation brought disaster. Even in summer, as General Karpunich describes, 'Prisoners were so hungry that at Zarosshy Spring they ate, in July, the carcass of a horse which had been lying for more than a week and which stank and was crawling with flies and worms. At the Utinyi prisoners ate half a barrel of grease which had been brought to oil the wheelbarrows. At Mylga they fed on moss, like reindeer.'[8]

The spring thaws might cut a camp off, as with the Spokoiny mine in the Northern Administration in May 1944, where mass death ensued. In winter, as General Karpunich tells us,

When the passes were snowbound, at the outlying mines each prisoner received 100 grams of bread a day, and the shortfall in rations was never made up later. Numerous utterly exhausted prisoners who could not walk were dragged to work on sledges pulled by other equally exhausted prisoners whose legs were not so swollen. Any who lagged behind were beaten with sticks and bitten by dogs. When work had to be carried out at temperatures of 45°C. below zero the prisoners were forbidden to start a fire to warm themselves. (Criminals were allowed to.)[8]

Another account of the results of heavy snow describes how short a time—a few days—was necessary to ruin the already weakened miners:

Shortly before Christmas heavy snowfalls began, cutting off our mine completely from the rest of the Kolyma. There was so much snow that some mine workers were transferred to the work of clearing a road. In the meantime, the last food reserves for the prisoners were exhausted.

First of all, as usual, the salt disappeared, and in all the dishes we were served in the dining hall it was replaced by herring. Soup with herring, gruel with herring. Then the cereal gave out, and there was no more gruel. There remained only soup with bread, the soup consisting of nothing but water with a small mixture of flour. Then, for three days, all workers received only a half-pound of bread per person, and on the morning of the fourth day everyone received a double portion of the same soup instead of bread. On the following day again there was no bread.

Real famine set in at the mine. Five thousand men did not have a piece of bread. But everyone worked as usual—twelve hours a day. The prudent administration put all guards on duty, fearing a hunger rebellion. These fears were groundless—the browbeaten and worn-out men were incapable of any energetic action.

Exhausted by long years of half-starved existence and inhuman labour, people spent their last remnants of strength in working. And died. During those days the nameless graves under the hill swallowed fifteen or twenty men every day.

In the evening of the fifth day, barely dragging our feet, my team-mate and I went directly to the dining hall on returning from work. Alexeev's eyes were burning feverishly. We had just come into the mess hall when our nostrils were struck by the smell of meat. From the kitchen window we were given a plate of soup each, and what soup! Large chunks of meat floated in it. Alexeev began to gulp it down at once, but I was seized by a sudden suspicion, knowing that the roads had not yet been cleared. Since there were few people in the dining hall, I went to the window and called the cook, whom I knew, to ask what kind of meat it was. The cook laughed, immediately guessing my thought. His fat face shone. 'So, you are afraid it is human meat? No, not yet. Calm down and eat it. Today they slaughtered three horses at the stable. They say that one died himself, but what's the difference?'

I agreed that it made no difference and returned to the table to eat my portion with great relish. After supper we went to our tent to sleep.[23]

Even apart from these special disasters, the system easily got out of hand, with a resulting shortfall in production. Roy Medvedev tells us that in Kolyma, 'The exhaustion of prisoners was so great that in the first post-war years there were frequent cases of two thousand to three thousand enrolled men turning out about one hundred to work in the mines.'[16]

But even when the system was grinding on in fairly orderly fashion, the cycle sooner or later set in. —'The exhaustion of the prisoners brings about a slowing down in the output. When the output goes down, the guards begin to beat them with their rifle-butts, put them into solitary confinement and finally shoot them.'[2]

In any case, a prisoner who had been reduced to a virtual wreck in three or four weeks, and had then managed to keep going somehow from day to day, finally became incapable of further effort and found himself on starvation rations as a *dokhodyaga*—'goner'.

The word *dokhodyaga* . . . applied in the camps to the men who have been reduced to such a low level mentally and physically that even as workers they are of very limited value. The name *dokhodyaga* is derived from the verb *dokhodit* which means to arrive or to reach. At first I could not understand the connection, but it was explained to me: the *dokhodyagas* were '*arrivistes*', those who had arrived at socialism, were the finished type of citizen in the socialist society.

Little consideration was shown in the treatment of these *dokhodyagas*. They were being reprimanded constantly, and received frequent cuffs on the head from the camp officials and guards. . . . The *dokhodyagas* always gobbled up the entire day's bread ration at breakfast time.[23]

The physical and mental deterioration is reported with horror by all survivors.

Hunger produces strange behaviour. Half-mad, the hungry

look like normal people. If famine hasn't entirely consumed them they defend their rights with fury. Eternal quarrellers, desperate skirmishers, they fight continuously. Discussions arise on the most petty pretext. . . . The small ones try to trip their adversaries up, the big ones to knock them over by sheer weight. The bodies hit and bite each other . . . often only trying to show off to an audience which never separates the combatants.[28]

And again, 'In those days one often saw people in camp who stood on all fours, growling and rooting about in the filthy garbage near the tents and, especially near the kitchen, looking for anything even remotely edible and devouring it on the spot. They had become semi-idiots whom no amount of beating could drive from the refuse heaps.'[23]

As in all extreme situations, stimulants were as much desired as food. Tea, rarely obtainable, would be stewed to a palpitating concentration. 'Tobacco', a Soviet journalist tells us, 'was even more precious than bread, and was scrupulously shared out amongst the team. Taken in minute "pinches" it acted as a stimulant and was given by the team leader when one or other of the team was completely exhausted.'[29]

The authorities, as frantic as the prisoners to complete their own norms, used this and other incentives. On turning in a nugget of $1\frac{1}{2}$ kilograms to the authorities a group of prisoners were given two ounces of tobacco each, half a day off, and a dinner at the canteen which catered for the freely employed. (The foreman was furious for, as he explained with much vituperation, he could have made it more worth their while if the team had applied to him.)[29]

In another camp, in the rare event of anyone exceeding the norm, the reward was a small bottle of cheap eau de cologne to drink. There were always a certain number of alcoholics, astonishing as it may seem. Some would drink anything from turpentine to anti-freeze. Even filtered through bread or cotton wool, these often caused death or blindness. Others managed to establish relations with the medical orderlies, and obtain medicines supposedly containing alcohol.

The continuous exhaustion which led to the total obsession with food and the occasional stimulant was much increased by an almost total lack of rest days. 'One autumn day in the Great North, they gave us our first day's rest after six months of uninterrupted toil. Everyone wanted simply to lie down doing nothing . . . when, in the morning, the administration of the camp sent us out on a wood-collecting fatigue.'[28]

Nor were the barracks or huts in which prisoners spent their spare hours much of a refuge. Desperately overcrowded, with bunks three or four deep, they were often quite uninsulated (guards' huts had sawdust between two layers of boarding). And, ill-constructed as they were, the cracks and holes were usually stuffed with moss, rags or straw. Moreover, almost all the miners were afflicted by incontinence of urine. They would try, when sent to other camps, to get the lower bunks, in order to spare their colleagues. Where they were all together this was not possible.[28]

The stoves, too, were quite inadequate. It was a constant complaint that 'The barracks were not given enough heat, clothing would not dry out. In the fall they kept people, soaked to the skin, out in the rain and the cold to fulfil norms that such hopeless wrecks could never fulfil. . . . Prisoners were not dressed for the climate in the Kolyma region. They were given third-hand clothing, mere rags, and often had only cloth wrapping on their feet. Their torn jackets did not protect them from the bitter frost, and people froze in droves.'[36]

We have noted the revealingly vicious regulations which,

from 1937, practically forbade clothing adequate to the climate. Boots were the most troublesome, after Yezhov's order banning felt in favour of sacking and canvas. One type of these *burki*

were made of lightly padded and quilted sacking with high, wide tops that reach to the knee, the shoe itself being strengthened by oilcloth or artificial leather at the toe and heel. The sole is made of three cross-sections of rubber from worn-out automobile tires. The whole thing is fastened to the foot with strings and tied with string below the knee so that the snow does not get in. These *burki* are so roomy that you can wrap three footrags around each foot. After a day's use they become all twisted, and the flabby soles turn every which way. They absorb moisture with incredible speed, especially when the sacks of which they are made were used for bagging salt, and hold the moisture obstinately. During the eight months of winter, drying the *burki* is the prisoner's principal problem. They are so heavy that after a march of several miles from the camp to the place of work you can scarcely lift your feet, although your day's work is just beginning. Heavy nailed mountaineering shoes are like elegant dancing pumps compared to these *Che-te-se*, as the prisoners call them; it is the abbreviation for Chelyabinsk Tractor Factory.[13]

The later *burki* were

a sort of boot, an economic product dating from the war. They cut them in hundreds of thousands from canvas trousers. The sole was made with the same material sewn into several thicknesses. . . . They also gave us strips of flannel. This is the way we went to work at the mines at 50° below and 60° below. After a few hours' work in the forest these *burki*, torn by the branches, came completely to pieces. In the mines the *burki* resisted for several days. Repairs were made rapidly by cobblers who worked through the night. In the morning the 'repairs' were done. They added successive layers of material for the sole, and the *burki* ended by being completely shapeless, like the churned-up bank of a mountain torrent after an avalanche.[28]

As for clothes—wadding jackets and trousers, a cloth cap with ear flaps (or shawl for women), cotton underwear, wadded mittens—all usually in rags. A Polish prisoner says: 'In winter, one has to work even in 65°C. of frost. Clothes get worn out very quickly in the mines. We went about wrapped in rags which we almost never took off; only very rarely in the bath-house. The ice-bound rags on our feet would thaw out in the vapour. After the bath, we had to wrap our feet again in these sodden rags.'[2]

The men did indeed need baths, and the clothes needed the disinfestation, which theoretically took place at the same time. Lice abounded. There were camps 'where they bathe every six months'. A doctor complaining of vermin would be told 'Were you ever at the Fifty-sixth Kilometre?—That's where you would see lice, my friend. . . .'[13]

But the bath and disinfestation procedure, which one might think so welcome to the prisoner, was on the contrary regarded as 'unjust'. 'When they [i.e. the politicals] moan about injustice, it's because the chief is sending them to the baths.'

Shalamov develops the point.

The rejection of the bath always astonishes the doctors and the administration, who see in this absenteeism an opposition to rules and a defiance of discipline. . . . Special gangs are formed: all the bosses participate personally in the hunt for abstainers. And the doctors too. The baths and the disinfestation of clothing are a direct part of their professional duties. . . . Special measures are enforced for such days (there are three a month). . . .

Why? Is it possible for a man, however miserable he may be, to refuse to wash, to get rid of the sweat and the filth which cover a body devoured by skin diseases; refuse to smell clean even if only for an hour? A Russian proverb actually says 'Happy as if just out of the bath'. Is one better with lice or without? And lice pullulate. Only disinfestation can get rid of them. . . .

Of course, lice are a relative matter. A dozen lice in one's underclothes don't count. Lice begin to attract the attention of the prisoners and doctors when one can shake them out with a movement of the hand, when a crawling pullover starts to move on its own. Is it possible that a man, of whatever type, might not wish to escape this torture when he does not sleep and scratches his filthy body, gnawed by vermin, till the blood runs?

No, of course not. But there is a 'but'. On bath days there's no spare time allotted. You go before or after work. After long hours in the cold (and the summer is no better) one wants only to plod to the barrack, swallow something and sleep. The baths delay this moment: it's unbearable. And the baths are always far from the camp, for they are used both by prisoners and by free employees. . . .

The bath and disinfestation don't take more than an hour. But there's the waiting. The prisoners arrive in large numbers, gang by gang. The late-comers wait outside, in the cold (they are taken direct from the place of work without going to the camp for fear that they would disperse and escape from control). When the cold is particularly intense, to save the prisoners too long a wait, they are allowed to go into the changing room designed for ten or fifteen people, where a hundred or so fully clothed men now cram themselves. . . . A fantastic hubbub, naked bodies and clothed bodies are mixed pell-mell, howling, shouting and stamping. Profiting from the noise and the confusion, the thieves steal their comrades' property, and as there are several brigades there, the stolen objects are never recovered. . . .

The second, or rather the third, 'but' is that on bath days a special gang, in the absence of the prisoners, carries out the cleaning of the barracks. They scrub, they wash, they mercilessly throw away everything superfluous. Now the least rag is precious when one thinks of the energy needed to acquire it: a pair of gloves or spare slippers, to say nothing of food or other objects, all disappear without trace and almost by regulation while the prisoners are at the baths.

To take one's personal objects to work and then to the bath is useless. The vigilant and experienced eyes of the common criminals are quick to notice this ruse. They can always exchange stolen gloves or slippers for a little tobacco.[28]

And then the bath itself:

A cup of lukewarm water and ice *ad lib.* (In the summer they give cold water instead of ice. All the same that's better.) Of course, a prisoner must know how to wash himself whatever the volume of water, a spoonful or a cistern. If he only has a spoonful he confines himself to his puss-caked eyes. . . .

There's a lack not only of water, of heat too. The stoves are not warm enough. There are cracks in the walls, draughts. . . . The bath-house is built directly on the moss. This dries out quickly and creates holes through which the cold comes in. Every bath brings the risk of frostbite. Everyone knows it, especially the doctors. Next morning the list of those off work for non-simulated illness is longer.

And besides, it is the prisoners themselves who have had to collect the wood the previous day and carry it on their shoulders, again holding up their return to barracks by several hours.

But still, that's nothing. The worst thing is the compulsory disinfestation. In camp, the underclothes can be 'individual' or 'collective'. These are official terms. . . . The individual underclothing, newer and stronger, is reserved for the administrative personnel, prisoner-bosses and other privileged ones. . . . The 'collective' underclothing is distributed on the spot, immediately after the bath, in exchange for the dirty underclothes which have been collected. The question of sizes does not arise. The clean underclothes are strictly a lottery. I've seen adults crying with rage when, in exchange for dirty, good underclothes, they've had clean, rotted underclothes. Nothing can take a man away from the contradictions which are the frame of his existence. Neither the fact that he won't have this underclothing longer than the next bath time nor that the good stuff was no more than a lucky chance, nor that the bad stuff isn't anything, after all, compared with a lost life. But they argue and cry. A sign of the psychological anomaly, of the 'dementia' which characterises almost all the actions of the prisoner. A universal malady . . . They argue, they speak of the underclothes they got last time and of those which were distributed five years ago at Bamgala.

The new underclothing is often damp. There hasn't been time to dry it for want of wood. They have to put it on immediately after the bath. . . . Clad in sodden underclothing, completely frozen, the prisoners have to wait further till their main clothing is disinfested.

Success in this depends on luck and on the goodwill of the man in charge. At best, only the clothes hung near the stove get the heat. Those behind get the damp, and those in the furthest corners remain cold. This disinfestation, which doesn't eliminate the vermin, exists only for the form and constitutes an additional torment to the prisoner. Doctors know this well. But you can't decently leave a camp without a disinfestation room. Finally, after an hour's wait in the changing room, the prisoners conclude their business with a pile of indistinguishable clothes thrown pell-mell on to the ground. Everyone, cursing, pulls out his coat, his undercoat, his cotton trousers, damp and smoky. Now you have to stay up the rest of the night to dry them out by the barrack stove.[28]

A woman prisoner confirms the inefficiency of disinfestation; 'the temperature was never brought up to the 100°C. which is necessary to kill the lice. Usually the heat in disinfestation chambers was just right to make the lice feel comfortable and stimulated.' She adds that, when it had become clearly impossible to delouse themselves, women would give up trying, and only when the itching became intolerable would reach under their blouses, 'fish out a handful of the vermin, and throw them away'.[13]

The whole question of health and hygiene was crucial to life in Kolyma. The lice, as we have seen, produced outbreaks of typhus. And when such sicknesses were added to the deficiency diseases which were universal in the camps, the prisoner who enjoyed even passable health for any length of time became almost a forgotten memory.

On arrival each prisoner had, of course, been given a medical check and been put into one of three categories—Heavy Physical Labour, Medium Physical Labour, and Light Physical Labour. But, in the first place, no one was rejected as unfit and the check consisted of three applications of the stethoscope—to the lungs and heart—plus an examination of the buttock muscles. All 'Trotskyites' were in any case sent to Heavy Labour. Moreover, commandants rarely paid attention to the categories because they had no light labour available, what there was being pre-empted by *urkas*.

Since the health of even genuinely strong and fit men could not stand work at the mines, the true distinction soon became simply between those whose bodies were irreversibly ruined and those who might yet recover if saved in time. The existence of sickness, even of the deficiency diseases caused directly by the system itself, was more or less recognised. Partly hypocrisy, partly formalism, partly mere double-think kept a retinue of doctors, infirmaries, hospitals going.

To go sick, anyway, required a temperature of at least 40°C., and was then only possible if the quota for sick that day had not been filled.[2] This quota (for 'P'—provisionally off work) was strictly limited at every level 'for each medical centre and for each ambulance service. No medical orderly or doctor dared exceed this norm, and risk being sent back to the mines.'[28]

There were the usual administrative difficulties. At Khatenakh

Even in cases of patent sickness, it was not always possible to get release from work. Patients were admitted to the dispensary only after 8 p.m. when men were beginning to return to the camp, and examinations took place for only two hours although sometimes there were over a hundred waiting. In addition, the camp commander limited release notes to from twenty to twenty-five a day, and if this number had been reached, a man was driven to work even if he had pneumonia and a temperature of 105°.[23]

Criminals had various methods of getting ill—drinking salt water, stealing a syringe from the infirmary and injecting kerosene under their skins, putting a wet rag on one of their feet or hands to get frostbite, cutting off their middle fingers, rubbing substances into the eye to produce symptoms like those of trachoma. They had a recipe, still believed to be secret, for producing the symptoms of syphilis. It was also possible to produce fevers and heart murmurs from particularly strong infusions of tea and tobacco. Sciatica was also faked, as of course were insanity and paralysis—though not often successfully. Prisoners with particularly large boils due to scurvy were 'particularly envied'.[13]

One form of self-mutilation was most remarkable. 'If a criminal has an idea that the new camp will be worse for him than his present one, he will at the last moment cut open the surface of his abdomen. Criminals are so skilful at this that they never injure their internal organs. In fact, such cases are so frequent that the prisoner is not even sent to the hospital. The gaping wound is sewed up in the camp infirmary, and if the criminal has bad luck he will at most gain half an hour by his self-mutilation. Then he will be tossed into the truck. . . .'[13]

Proved cases of malingering and self-mutilation were punishable, but doctors rarely made such a report if there was any way to avoid it. There was the regulation that self-mutilators were allowed no more than thirteen days in hospital, but this too was generally evaded.

In genuine illness it was in general 'only when the doctors themselves were prisoners'[36] that some real help might be available. Even so, they risked their own appointments, and hence their lives, by their attitudes. One actually slipped some vitamin C syrup, a packet of butter and a 25 rouble note into the pocket of a sick prisoner whom he could not otherwise help.[31]

But there were also a number of 'free' doctors not belonging to the NKVD, who maintained their humanity. Shalamov, describing the horror of such a doctor, just come back from the front, when faced with the state of the prisoners, says he was reminded of General Ridgway's remarks after the war, when the American troops entered the Nazi camps: 'The experience of a soldier at the front cannot prepare one for the spectacle of death in the camps.'[28]

Normally, the treatment available in camp was anyhow of little use. One prisoner writes that at his camp, the dispensary only had iodine and soda.[23] Another describes when he was in an extremely sick condition, that every time he went to the doctor 'the doctor threw into my mouth a great spoonful of permanganate, and shouted, turning away, "Next"'. Permanganate was the all-purpose medicine, the only one in use at the camp. 'They gave it to you to drink for dysentery, poured it over frostbite, wounds and burns.'[28] (Frostbite, usually contracted not at work but when standing outside to be mustered and counted, was common. It is reported that through the winter 10 to 15 per cent of the prisoners got serious frostbite needing treatment.)[13]

As for getting into the infirmary attached to most large camps, as Mrs Ginzburg puts it, 'As a rule the infirmary took in only those who were plainly dying and not all of them.'[4]

There were enough exceptions to support the hospital system. This was based on the thousand-bed Central Hospital, which was in Magadan until the war, when it was moved twice, each time further north; and in addition there were small local hospitals in the Administrations.

Apart from physical cases, there was a high incidence of madness. Psychiatric cases seemed, at least after the war, to have been treated as well as was feasible, both in special barracks near Magadan and at a four-storey building at Kilometre 500 on the Kolyma.

The normal sick who made good progress in hospital were sent to 'invalid camps': 'In the Kolyma region there were so-called *slabosilki*, where they kept convalescents after discharge from the hospital. Here they were confined for three weeks. The ration was indeed better: 700 grams of bread. But three weeks for a wreck were the same as a bone for a hungry dog. I regarded those infirmaries as a way of covering up. . . . As if to say, "we took suitable measures, but they did not want to work and live."'[36]

From these 'invalid camps'—one of which was at Kilometre 23 until moved out to Kilometre 72— 'every morning several corpses are taken out.'[13] And the hospitals and infirmaries remained under pressure to supply labour. For example at the beginning of the digging season in the spring, the chief of the Northern Administration would arrive at the local hospital with guards to take off all prisoners who could stand.[13]

Those prisoners who did not get re-categorised as suitable for physical labour were now divided into two groups—'Working Invalids' and 'Non-Working Invalids'. There were sometimes posts for the former, on low rations. For example, at Elgen:

In every barrack an elderly woman, medically certified as

an invalid, was on barrack duty. She swept and washed the floor, fetched and carried drinking water and water for washing, carried out used water and refuse, kept the stoves burning and, with the aid of inmates who took turns helping her, sawed and split the firewood. She brought food to the sick who were temporarily excused from work, collected dirty wash once a month and took it to the prison laundry outside the camp, brought back the laundry and distributed it. Her bread ration was 17½ ounces when the top ration for prisoners was 21 ounces: when the top ration was reduced to 17½ ounces, in 1941–3, she received 14 ounces, and no pay at all from the camp. But it was customary for the other inmates of the barrack to make a voluntary collection every month, so that she usually received more money than any of the other prisoners. All knew that what few decencies of life they had in the camp depended upon this old woman. Everyone was grateful to her. When we came back to the barrack, soaking wet, frozen, and exhausted, she was there to welcome us with a friendly, maternal smile. She contrived to steal a little extra firewood somewhere in the camp—the official ration of wood was always ridiculously small; she saw to it that the 'tea' was hot and in adequate quantity; and she did not fuss overmuch about the snow that everyone tracked into the barrack. And it was she who awoke us in the morning when we stubbornly refused to hear the bell for rising.[13]

Many 'Working Invalids' had less luck. A Soviet writer describes how

One morning a party arrived at the camp made up of men who had been worked to exhaustion in the mines and were no longer any good for underground operations. On their march back they had died—I was going to say like flies—but at Kolyma it was truer to say that the flies died like people.

The survivors were sorted out at Magadan, where a few remained. The rest were sent on, for allegedly light work, to such places as the Taskan food plant where, before being released to a better world, they performed the noble task of developing the food supplies by spending 12 hours a day in 60° of frost in the forest, cutting the branches of *stlannik* on which the factory depended for its raw material.[4]

As for the 'Non-Working Invalids', on minimum rations, they pottered around the camps doing odd jobs till they died. In their cases, dystrophy had become irreversible and they were *dokhodyagas*.

Going sick, in any case, usually led in one way or another to the vicious circle of cut rations, which ended in death. General Gorbatov gives the general attitude: 'What were we to do? We couldn't say that we were ill: they would just cut our bread ration. What medicine would they give us, anyway? There was only one medicine to be had—an infusion of pine needles. Beyond that there was only one alternative—six feet under. So pull, comrade, pull while you still can.'[5]

The pine infusion Gorbatov speaks of was that supplied by the 'light work' prisoners at Taskan. It was compulsory to drink the concentrate before meals.[13] It was supposed to combat scurvy, a result of vitamin C deficiency (just as a prisoner actually suffering from pellagra had to give up 1.75 ounces of his bread ration in favour of a yeast concoction). If pure it caused severe pain and was rejected by many prisoners, being eventually (1954) abandoned.[31]

Meanwhile an attempt had been made to find a superior substitute in the leaves of the dwarf willow, which were also processed at the Vitamin Combine. One prisoner involved in collecting there remarks:

I went on an expedition with a 'vitamin' gang, ordered to collect the leaves of dwarf willows, the only plant that is always green in these regions. The leaves were carried hundreds of versts to the Vitamin Combine where they were cooked into a thick brown broth of nauseating taste and odour. . . . The doctors used it as one of the main compulsory treatments for the scurvy that then ravaged the camps, and at the same time pellagra and the other vitamin deficiencies. Anyone who swallowed even a drop of this diabolical drug agreed that death was better. But an order is an order. In the camp the authorities didn't distribute the rations until the patients had swallowed this potion. . . . Dinner, to which the prisoner attached so much value, was irretrievably spoilt by this obligatory aperitif. This went on for more than ten years. Doctors, who had received some instruction, were astounded that this willow broth could still contain vitamin C, which is extremely sensitive to changes of temperature. In fact, they knew that the broth had no virtue at all, but the distribution continued. . . . It wasn't till after the war that the medical authorities of the region sent the administration of the camp an order categorically forbidding the use of the dwarf willow leaves extract. It appeared that it had catastrophic effects on the kidneys. They shut the Combine.[28]

This curious attempt to prevent one of the plagues which were the natural and normal result of the whole Kolyma system of feeding is reported by prisoner after prisoner.

The struggle to avoid the minimum ration and irrevocable sickness was, as we have seen, complicated by the fact that one could miss a maximum ration not only by the mere failure of one's effort to fulfil a norm, but also by incurring the 'disciplinary' ration—that is, by infringing some rule, or merely offending some official. There were, of course, offences punishable by death and there were times when an offence previously incurring a smaller sentence became capital. For example:

Refusal to work is punished by a sentence in the lockup. A notation of the case is made and signed by the camp commander, the commander of the guard, and the doctor. From three to five such notations are sufficient to bring a work-shirker to trial. In peacetime he was given additional sentences of from five to ten years on the basis of Paragraph 58, Article 14: counter-revolutionary sabotage. During wartime counter-revolutionaries who refused to work were shot; criminals usually got off with an additional sentence of ten years.[13]

Concealing gold was almost always a capital offence. Previous to 1938 there had been a money premium for nuggets over 50 grams. This was changed to an offer of a gram of alcohol for every gram of gold in nuggets over 100 grams—an inadequate return, which led to cases 'where prisoners who found big nuggets threw them away into the bushes rather than hand them over to the authorities. They were put to death, but it did not make the prisoners any more keen on looking for nuggets.'[23]

Mere suspicion, on the other hand, was one of those considerations which might involve not a death sentence as such, but a session in the camp lockup. A Soviet-published account tells of an episode when a team had been accused of concealing gold which they had found. Their quarters were thoroughly searched but nothing was found. However, in order to 'teach the men a lesson', the whole team had been sentenced to solitary confinement in a section known as 'Stalin's villa'. Only a few of the team survived the experience and returned to work.[29]

Again,

Nothing was easier than to get into the punitive cell because of the *zachistka*, i.e. the clearing up of the soil after a gold-bearing stratum had been exploited. This work consisted of sweeping a strip of land of 36 square metres and brushing it with small brushes so that no traces of gold could be found. . . . It often happened that the ore with tiny grains of gold was deeply embedded in the earth and had to be dug out and carried on wheelbarrows to a designated place. In other instances there were holes filled with water and gravel. After many cubic metres of sludge had been excavated from the hole, examination would still reveal the presence of gold: the soil had not been properly dealt with, and the prisoner usually landed in the cells.[18]

Sometimes,

a brigade which had not fulfilled the norm had to work throughout the night and then continue the following day, without rest or food, so as to deliver the required amount of gold. Prisoners who did not reach the prescribed norm were put, right after work, into a punitive cell. Before entering it, the prisoner had to take off all his clothes except his underwear. He had to spend the night in a wooden barrack, with rain, snow, or frost penetrating through the cracks in the walls. I personally was able to take it because I had wrapped a towel around my chest, underneath my shirt, with which I covered myself and a companion. Towards morning, we would hear cries emanating from the cell: 'Open the door, chief, I am dying.' After emerging the prisoner had to resume his habitual place and work the whole day, along with the others.[18]

For these lockups, the 'Stalin villas', were an essential in every camp. A woman prisoner lists the misdemeanours for which lockup was the usual punishment:

Lateness in leaving camp for work; talking while going out to work; impertinence to the guards, camp administrators or other free citizens; smoking in the barracks; smoking while going out to work; wearing unauthorised clothing (say, private coats or shoes); leaving the place of work without permission; being found with a man, even though it is in a harmless conversation, which it usually is not; entering a house or store in a free settlement; drunkenness; bringing food back into camp; disorder in the barracks; disorderly cot; refusal to work; theft in camp; theft at the place of work; failure to meet labour quota; use of unauthorised places as a latrine; fighting among prisoners (guards who beat prisoners receive no punishment); refusal to take part in extra duty or shock-troop work (*udarniki*) for the camp, that is, work which must be done after the end of the official twelve-hour working day; leaving the barracks, except to go to the latrine, after the evening roll call; washing laundry in the barracks, washing hair in the barracks; burning holes in clothing, and so forth.

'In a camp with several hundred inmates, not a day passes without some sentences to the lockup. At one time or another every prisoner receives a lockup sentence. . . .'

The lockup itself was

usually without windows, without illumination, and un-heated or very inadequately heated. Frozen toes among the prisoners are frequently due to a stay in the lockup. It contains a biggish common cell and a few tiny solitary cells, the usual planks and the usual bedbugs and lice. . . . The camp commanders hand out lockup sentences of from one to ten days for a great variety of infractions of camp discipline; only in very severe cases is the sentence for twenty days. You can be sentenced to the lockup with or without permission to work. The latter type is the harsher sentence. If the prisoner is let out to work he can usually manage to get a little more food than he is allotted, and above all, by moving around at work he can warm up more easily than he can in the lockup.[13]

There were other, irregular, punishments as well as these highly correct and institutional ones. A Soviet general tells that his camp chief

punished those who did not fulfil their norms in the following ways: in winter the prisoner was stripped naked at the mine face, cold water was poured over him and he was left to run back to the camp. In summer the prisoner would again be stripped naked, his hands tied behind him to a common pole and all those so fixed would be put out into a cloud of mosquitoes. (The guard wore a mosquito net over his head.) Finally, the prisoners were also simply beaten with rifle butts and flung into the cooler.[8]

A Pole recounts how 'one of my fellow workers, Untenberg, a German from the Volga district, who had not fulfilled his norm of output, was ordered by the guard to undress and to stay naked without budging. The night was clear, . . . and swarms of mosquitoes covered his body. In the morning he was all swollen, he screamed from pain and rolled on the ground despite the order not to move.'[18]

In addition to these disciplinary sanctions, the guards carried out investigative checks. Above all, there were constant searches, much loathed by the prisoners. As one points out, 'Rich or poor, prisoners or otherwise, every man quickly accumulates a lot of odd objects. . . . It's the same for a prisoner: he's a worker, he must have a needle, a bit of cloth to mend his clothes. . . . Everything's thrown away and every time those who haven't managed to hide their stuff in the snow for 24 hours have to start all over again.'[28]

A woman says that these searches

are an important part of life both in prisons and camps. Female prisoners may be searched only by women. Since there are usually not enough women supervisors in the camps, the camp administration also uses prisoners who are in turn checked upon by soldiers of the guard. There is a shake-down every time the prisoners re-enter the camp, that is, once or twice a day. In addition at least every two months there is a thorough search of the barrack and of all the prisoners' belongings. This operation is always carried out in the middle of the night and usually lasts several hours. Suddenly the entire barrack will be full of guards who chase the frightened women off the planks and begin rummaging through bundles and mattresses in all corners of the barrack at once, so that the prisoners cannot pass things around to conceal them. Nevertheless, almost all the prisoners own a home-made knife fashioned out of a piece of sharpened iron. At night this is carefully stuck into a crack between the planks. The reason for this is that you can make your bread ration go farther by cutting it into slices than by breaking off pieces.

Shake-downs are particularly rigid before and during the state holidays on 1 May and 7 November; apparently the administration then fears some demonstration on the part of the prisoners, although the idea of a demonstration on these or any other days never even enters the prisoners' heads. The two cases of genuine counter-revolutionary demonstrations which took place in two women's camps were carried out, significantly enough, by criminals. They hung up a placard reading, 'Long live fascism!' They were shot, and their names and the announcements of the executions were read to us at the evening roll call.

Ordinarily the guards turn up scarcely anything in the course of these searches: writing paper, pencils, cotton bags, home-made sewing needles, contraband food which may have been bought with endless trouble and excitement from the earnings of two or three months, and money in excess of fifty roubles. For there is a regulation that no prisoner may have in his possession more than fifty roubles—even though he may have been paid more than that in wages. What we hated worse than the coarseness of the guards, worse than the confiscation of the little things we needed, worse than the humiliation of the whole procedure, was the fact that we were robbed of our all-too-brief night's sleep. For all through the years in camp we suffered from chronic fatigue.[13]

In cases where some stoolpigeon had definitely reported an illegal object, which the guards nevertheless could not find, traditional NKVD methods were used. At the Novaya Zyryanka prison in 1938, a prisoner was held in a straitjacket in icy conditions for a day, to locate a real knife.[38]

But the main application of 'interrogation' procedures was in the work of the Third Section of the NKVD, which had to produce new charges and sentences for those whose term was theoretically approaching its close. Very complex frame-ups, with days of standing and sleeplessness, are reported especially in 1938—for example, when at the Lobuya camp a geologist, an airman and others were so treated, and also beaten, at various periods over several months, to confess to a local counter-revolutionary plot.[38]

Later an easier routine was followed. 'It was a thoroughly everyday matter: those in charge of the work force went through the filing cards looking for prisoners who were approaching the end of wastefully short sentences, summoned them in bundles of 80 – 100 men at a time and added a new 10-year sentence to each of them.'[26]

One peculiarity marked the relation of jailer and prisoner in Kolyma compared with the camps of the 'mainland': the precautions against escape were small; and escape—of sorts—took place. Though security at the camp sites was laxer, and prisoners were allowed out on their own on 'woodcutting' parties, for example. Kolyma itself in its distances and isolation constituted one vast prison. Almost without exception 'they are caught, a few days or a few weeks later. . . .

'The innumerable camp guards, the operational units aided by thousands of German shepherd dogs, the detachments of frontier guards and the troops called the "Kolyma Regiment" are enough to catch the prisoners without exception. The upkeep of a corps of "headhunters" is less expensive to the country than the upkeep of jailers.'[28]

Urkas seldom escaped;

'they didn't believe escape possible. The police and the camp guards, rich in long experience, had a sixth sense in recognising them. The police claimed that men of that class are marked with an indelible seal. This sixth sense showed itself one day. A criminal, sentenced for theft and murder, had escaped. He was armed. He was searched for for more than a month all over Kolyma.

The soldier Sevastianov stopped an unknown in a

sheepskin coat near a petrol station at the edge of the road. The man turned and Sevastianov shot him in the forehead. He hadn't seen the thief's face for this happened in winter and the fugitive was muffled up. The description Sevastianov had was vague (it isn't possible to verify everyone's tattoo). The photo he had of the bandit was dark and blurred. But his instincts had not deceived him.

From the dead man's coat, a rifle fell. A revolver was found in his pocket. He had adequately convincing papers. What should one think of the energetic conclusion dictated by this sixth sense? One moment more and it would have been Sevastianov who would have been shot down.[28]

For politicals too, the motivation to escape back to the USSR was low.

Escape where? To their families, to their friends? In 1938 the first passer-by they looked at on the road would himself have fallen under repression. It wasn't a question of their own fifteen or twenty years, it was the life of their relatives which was threatened. Someone would have had to have helped the fugitive and hidden him. In 1938, for the political prisoners, no one would have taken the risk. If a prisoner ever went back having served his sentence, which was very rare, his wife checked if his papers were in order and ran as quickly as the concierge did to report to the police. . . .

Nothing remained for them but to die and they died without thinking of escaping. They died, showing once again this national quality which Tyutchev has glorified, and which all politicians have abused—patience.[28]

All the same, in spring the escapes would start. The authorities increased the number of guards and dogs, and trained and drilled them. The escapers—few but determined—had food and made plans. If they were caught in the immediate search by their own camp guards, they

were not often captured alive. The taste for human blood sharpened the hatred of the guard for the prisoner.

Prisoners feared for their lives above all during transfers. . . . One imprudent word could send you into the other world. This is why prisoners asked to have their hands tied behind their back. There was then less risk of having written into your file the . . . phrase 'Killed while attempting to escape'. The enquiry was quick. If the killer had had the intelligence to fire a second shot into the air, he risked nothing. The regulation was that the first shot should be fired into the air. . . .[28]

Once away, a new world opened. Most of them hardly even planned on more than a few days' liberty. They hid in caves and abandoned bears' dens, having taken what they could, sometimes managing to break into the camp stores on the night of their departure. Even those who were not able to take much planned to live on the country—not on roots and berries, but on stealing from passing food lorries as they laboured up hills. When this practice started, lorries were often convoyed, but not always.

'The cold of the following winter invariably forced them back, unless they preferred dying of cold to long days in the punishment cells, long beatings, hunger, sometimes death.'[28]

One man, at Olchan, escaped down the Indigirka River on two logs, reaching the Arctic Ocean where he was, of course, recaptured. On another occasion, near Elgen, in 1947, an ex-officer being marched in a column of prisoners disarmed and shot both the guards and escaped with their rifles and ammunition, killing and wounding several pursuers before shooting himself.[32]

Of a number of recorded cases of escapes, two deserve reference. One was a mass escape by imprisoned army officers after the war.

Lieutenant-Colonel Yanovsky was now Prisoner Yanovsky, the 'cultural organiser' of an important camp section. This section had been formed immediately after the war from the soldiers of Vlasov, Russians who had gone over to the enemy, and the inhabitants of occupied villages suspected of collaboration.

These men had seen death face to face. They had the habit of war. The animal struggle for life, risks and death. They had already escaped from the Germans, the Russians, the English. . . . They'd often bet their lives on a coin. They were soldiers, men used to killing. Taught in a rough school, they continued to struggle for survival, this time against the State.

The authorities, who had hitherto only known the peaceful Trotskyites,could not suspect that these were men of action. One day an important personage visited the camp. Having looked into the life of the new ones and their work he remarked that their cultural and artistic activities left something to be desired. The former Lieutenant-Colonel Yanovsky, camp cultural organiser, replied respectfully: 'Don't worry, we will prepare a concert of which all Kolyma will talk.'

During the winter the prisoners, who were waiting for spring for their escape, took over, little by little, all the administrative posts. . . . All the civil personnel of the camp were chosen by Yanovsky in person. Airmen, drivers, electricians, they were all capable of assisting with the risks of an escape. The climatic and geological conditions were carefully studied. No one was blind to the difficulties of the enterprise. They had one aim: to live free, or die with arms and hands. They did not want to die of hunger on a camp bunk. Yanovsky knew that his comrades had to preserve their strength and keep up their morale. The prisoners he had put into these jobs ate well and did not weaken too quickly. . . .

At five o'clock in the morning exactly, someone knocked on the window. The sentry looked through the pane. It was the camp cook, Soldatov, who had come to get the key of the provision shed. Hung on a nail, this was inside the guard post. The cook had come to get this key every morning at five o'clock for months. The sentry unbarred the door and let Soldatov in. The other sentry had just gone out by the outside door. He lived with his family a few hundred metres from the post.

Everything had been calculated and the producer was looking through a little window at the first act he had planned for so long. . . .

The cook went to the wall where the key hung. There was another knock on the pane. The sentry knew well the man who knocked. It was Shetvtsov, the camp mechanic and armourer: he often repaired the machine carbines, the rifles and the pistols of the section. At this moment Soldatov threw himself on the sentry from behind and strangled him, with the help of Shetvtsov who had now entered. They hid the body under some logs. Soldatov put on the man's uniform, took the revolver and sat at the sentry's table. The other sentry came in. Before he could gather what had happened he had been strangled like the first. Shetvtsov put on his clothes.

The wife of the second sentry, the one who'd gone home, entered the post unexpectedly. They did not kill her. They tied her hands and feet and hid her with the bodies. The night shift came back to camp. The guard in charge of them came into the post. He too was killed. . . . Outside, life followed its usual course. It was the time of departure for work. The Lieutenant-Colonel took command of his men. . . .

Two guards gave orders, the team formed up. It was quite small: ten men. They marched off. They left the road and turned into a pathway. That didn't worry the sentries. Teams which were late often followed this route, which passed in front of the guards' barrack. . . . The sentry, half asleep, saw them from the opening of the door and had just time to ask why they were in Indian file and not in rank. He was surrounded and disarmed. The leader threw himself towards the pyramid of rifles piled near the sentry.

Armed with a machine pistol, Yanovsky opened the door of the barrack room where forty soldiers of the guard were sleeping. . . . A burst of fire through the ceiling made everyone lie on their bellies under the beds. He passed the gun to Shetvtsov and went out to the courtyard where his comrades were already collecting provisions and arms. . . .

Up on the guard posts the sentries had decided not to open fire. Later they said it was impossible to try and make out what was going on. Their word was not accepted and they were punished.

The fugitives did not hurry. Yanovsky organised the arms and ammunition. For food he recommended they should only take biscuits and chocolates. The medical orderly, Nikolsky, put individual packets in a sack marked with a red cross. . . . The telephone wires had been cut. By the time news reached the next camp, the fugitives had already got to the main road. They stopped the first empty lorry. The driver came out, covered by a revolver, and the war pilot, Kidalidze, took the wheel. The lorry headed towards Seimchan, the nearest airfield, to seize an aeroplane and fly off! . . .

After driving some way, they were fired on:

Yanovsky had foreseen this eventuality. Ten kilometres further on, Kidalidze stopped. The fugitives abandoned the lorry, jumped over the ditch and disappeared into the taiga. They were still 50 kilometres from the airfield. . . .

Next morning they came across soldiers who were searching the taiga. Four soldiers were killed at once. Yanovsky set fire to the forest: the wind was blowing towards the enemy. The fugitives went on.

But already lorries crammed with soldiers were pouring along the roads of Kolyma. Large numbers of regular troops came to reinforce the local garrisons and the special detachments. The Seimchan road was blocked every 10 kilometres. The highest authorities in Kolyma were personally conducting this exceptional operation. . . .

The evening of the second day, Yanovsky's group once again fell in with a patrol and had to fight. Ten soldiers were left dead. . . . The third night, . . . they were encircled. . . . The commander . . . waved a handkerchief and cried, 'Surrender, you are surrounded. Flight is impossible. . . .' He collapsed. . . . Shetvtsov had killed him with a bullet in the forehead . . . A new attack, a new repulse . . . They brought up two machine-guns. Yet another attack . . . They found only one survivor, the cook Soldatov, shot in both knees, the shoulder and the upper arm. Yanovsky and Kuznetsov had disappeared.

The same evening 20 kilometres away by river, they stopped an unknown soldier in uniform. Surrounded, he shot himself. It was Kuznetsov. There remained only the organiser, Lieutenant-Colonel Yanovsky. His fate remained mysterious. . . . They searched for months. . . . All the exits were guarded. He probably committed suicide in a cave or bear's den and his body was eaten by savage beasts. . . .

After the fight . . . 'What's happening here? Is there a war?' the surgeon asked the commander.

'It's not a war, but it's rather like it. I've had twenty-eight killed. And how many wounded you'll find out for yourself. As for me I'll lose my post. I'll have to make an unexpected retirement.' He was right. He lost his post and was transferred to another sector. Soldatov was condemned to 25 years. The camp commandant got 10 years; the sentries 5 years. In the mine more than 60 people were sentenced. Those who knew and had said nothing, those who had helped, those who thought of helping but hadn't had the time to do so. The garrison commandant would have been ruined for life if Shetvtsov's bullet hadn't saved him. Potapova, the chief doctor, was declared blame-worthy. The escaped medical orderly, Nikolsky, had worked under her. But she managed to get transferred very quickly and that saved her.[28]

All other escapes into the taiga were similarly unsuccessful—25 prisoners overpowering their guards on a lorry in early autumn, and all caught and being amputated for frostbite within four days; two army officers; two men who had taken a third to eat—an indictable offence. The only successful escape from Kolyma was conceived on different lines:

Krivoshey fled in the direction away from the sea, towards

Yakutsk. He was lightly laden. A thick raincoat, a geologist's hammer, a bag containing a few geological specimens, matches and money. Nothing else.

He didn't hide, he didn't rush. He followed horse tracks and deer paths. He passed in front of the rural police posts, went through villages, never wandered into the taiga, and slept every night under the roof of a cabin, tent or hut. In the first big settlement in Yakutia, he got workers, whom he paid, to dig little trenches—just what they'd already done for real geologists. He had the necessary technical knowledge: he had lived for nearly a year at Arkagala, an important geological base, and he had observed the behaviour of geologists. The weighty gestures, the tortoise-shell glasses, the daily shave, the well-tended finger-nails, inspired limitless confidence.

Krivoshey did not hurry. He inscribed mysterious signs in his road book, as he'd seen geologists do. Slowly but surely he went on towards Yakutsk.

Sometimes, even, he went back on his tracks, made a detour, slowed up. To confuse his tracks, he went through the semblance of exploring the basin of the Ryabaya. Krivoshey had nerves of steel. . . . After a month he crossed the crest of the Yablonov. Two Yakuts sent by a collective farm to accompany this important state mission carried the bag of 'specimens'. . . . At Yakutsk, Krivoshey went to the geological centre and asked for their help in sending some very important packages to the Academy of Sciences in Moscow. He went to the baths, to the hairdresser. He bought an expensive suit, several coloured shirts, underwear, dyed his hair and presented himself with a debonair smile to the Director of Scientific Research. He was very well received. His knowledge of foreign languages produced the desired effect.

Seeing in the newcomer a man of high culture, not so common in the streets of Yakutsk at that time, they begged him to prolong his stay. Pavel Mikhailovich replied with confusion that he had to get back rapidly to Moscow. The Director promised to pay his trip as far as Vladivostok. . . . He added, 'You will not refuse, my dear colleague, to give one or two lectures to our prospectors on any subject you like. . . .' 'Oh, certainly, with great pleasure. Within the limits of what is permitted to be divulged. You yourself will understand that information . . . without Moscow's permission . . .' The lecture took place, before a good number of listeners. . . . The guest from Moscow got as far as Irkutsk on the fees from the scientific bodies of Yakutsk.

'The strangest thing', Krivoshey used to tell us, 'is that during the three months my trip took, no one anywhere asked me for my papers.'. . .

He ended up at Mariupol, bought a house and got a job thanks to his false documents.

Krivoshey's wife had left Kharkov to join him. . . . Of course, she did not find work at Arkagala. She left it for Magadan, capital of the territory, where she found a job. . . . When Krivoshey escaped they thought he would hide with his wife. She was arrested but nothing could be got out of her. . . . They did not let her go back to the mainland. Authorisations to leave were given by the very organs which were searching for her husband. Such cases had been foreseen. She settled down to wait. The months went by. She still received refusals without explanation. She was shut in an immense stony prison covering one eighth of the Soviet Union which she could not leave. . . .

Her husband had earlier often repeated to her the phrase of a German general: 'War is won by the man with the firmest nerves.' She whispered these words during the white polar nights when she felt that her nerves were giving way. She was troubled for her husband. . . . Perhaps he had died of hunger on the way or been killed by other fugitives or by soldiers. The only thing that reassured her was the constant surveillance of which she was the object. She deduced from it that her husband had not been caught, that they were still searching for him, and she was happy not to be suffering for nothing.

She wanted to confide in someone. . . . But in whom? She felt in everyone a spy ready to denounce her and she was right. All her acquaintances had been called in and warned.

They waited for her confidences with impatience. During her second year of surveillance, she tried to get in touch through friends in Kharkov. Her letters were intercepted.

Reduced to misery, half-mad, only knowing that her husband was alive and that she should join him, she sent letters Poste Restante to all the big towns in the name of Pavel Mikhailovich Krivoshey.

In reply she got a postal order, then other small sums—500 or 800 roubles a month. The place of despatch and the despatchers varied. Krivoshey was too intelligent to send the money from Mariupol, and the administration was too experienced not to understand this. They marked out an area of manoeuvre on a staff map. The pins indicating the places from which the money had been sent followed the line of the railway from Mariupol to the north. . . . They checked the names of the people who had arrived in Mariupol during the last two years, compared photographs. Pavel Krivoshey was arrested.

What was his mistake? This escape had used all human qualities: talent, tenacity, subtlety, physical endurance. It was an escape without precedent in the care taken in its preparation, in the psychological depths and finesse that it showed. An astonishing escape because it only required a very small number of lies, the test of its success. An extraordinary escape: for the first time, one man had entered into a struggle with the State and its thousands of armed men in a territory where, since the time of the Tsars, fugitives had been given up for white flour at a rate of eight kilograms a head—after the Revolution this tariff was actually the subject of a legislative measure. Rightly seeing in every individual an informer and a coward, he had fought alone and he had won.

His wife had been a faithful and courageous companion. It was she who had brought the papers and money—more than 50,000 roubles—to Arkagala. With her husband arrested they let her leave at once. Morally and physically exhausted, she left Kolyma by the first boat.[28]

An exploit worth recounting, unique, and finally

abortive. Escape, even temporarily, was the rare adventure of a few—almost always newly arrived convicts still not physically broken. Death was the most usual relief from the camps. But, of course, the fact of our having evidence of all this is a sign that there was another possibility—survival.

Survivors make it clear, first of all, that it was essential to avoid being kept in the mines. No survivors did an uninterrupted stint of more than a few months in those conditions. Shalamov's view is that 'it took twenty to thirty days to turn a healthy man into a wreck.' General Gorbatov, a man of great strength and vigour, barely survived such a stint. Though mines varied to some extent, it is a rule that all survivors are men who managed to obtain other jobs. The same is true of the women survivors, none of whom worked continually at the manual jobs of Elgen and the hard-labour camps. In fact, it appears to be an invariable rule that whenever we come across anyone who has survived a really long period as a prisoner in Kolyma, it is because he or she has been able to obtain a 'function'—in an office, as a nurse, and so on, not only escaping the excessive labour of the main body of the work force but also, generally speaking, having better access to food.

A shorter stay, of course, increased the chance of survival. Gorbatov was only in Kolyma for about a year. Several witnesses are Poles, released after the outbreak of the Soviet–German war in 1941. And a further thing which greatly improved the chances of survival was to have been sent to Kolyma before the end of 1937. Prisoners who had arrived in the earlier period had the advantage of getting acclimatised, learning the conditions and making connections. When the terror wave broke in 1937–8, they were better equipped to resist it than the disorientated masses of the new intake—most of whom, at this period, were in any case from Party, administrative and similar jobs and quite unused to hard manual labour. Moreover they were, of course, fresh from intensive months of physical and psychological debilitation. Above all, over the few weeks of back-breaking labour which reduced them to wrecks, the new intake never had time to learn how to cope with the system and the climate.

One notes of the old-timers,

These were men that had already spent one or more winters there. They were incomparably cleaner. Even in the extremely harsh conditions of their life in camp they had managed to wash their faces every day, and when they could not get water, they had used snow. They were better dressed, too, thanks to the better clothes they had been able to preserve somehow from the old pre-Pavlov days. These old-timers were more self-possessed. They did not crowd about the stoves, but sat on their bunks either doing something or talking about their affairs. Even from the outside their tent looked different. You realised that the men who lived there tried by themselves, as far as they could, to make the tent warmer by covering it with moss and snow.[23]

In a sense, they were better adjusted; but this included being simply more vigilant. For to save one's life meant to be alert and decisive in a dozen incidents and contexts day after day. The right reaction to an *urka* might be crucial.

The boss, a lively and energetic type, looked young but he went round the ranks of his new workers with an experienced eye. My scarf interested him immediately. It was cotton of course, not wool, but it was a scarf, a free man's scarf. A hospital orderly had given it me as a present the previous year and ever since I'd worn it round my neck summer and winter. I washed it as I could when we went to the 'baths'. I didn't give it in for disinfestation even though it was full of lice, because one can't have everything and they would have stolen it from me immediately. My colleagues in the barracks, the boys with whom I lived and worked, hunted the scarf within the rules. The others did it outside these rules. Who doesn't want to get something with which he can buy tobacco and bread? Any free man would have bought this scarf. It's easy to get rid of lice by putting it through steam. It's only difficult for a prisoner. But I heroically wound my scarf around my neck before going to sleep. I tied it at the throat in spite of the intolerable lice. One doesn't get any more accustomed to lice than to cold.

'You'll sell it?' the fellow said.

'No.'

'As you wish . . . you've no need of a scarf.'. . .

Without looking at anyone he read out names in a monotonous tone and quoted for each the amount of work done as compared with the norm. Then he folded his paper carefully and went out. The barrack was silent. One could only hear the breathing of several dozen men in the gloom.

'The last name', my neighbour explained, 'won't have bread tomorrow.'

'No bread at all?'

'None.'

I'd never seen that anywhere. In the mines, the ration depended on the work of the brigade taken as a whole. At worst one got the penal ration, that is 300 grams. But they never suppressed bread entirely. . . .

I understood why there was this list of percentages. . . . he had not forgotten my scarf. . . .

'Sell me your scarf.'

'I had it as a present, citizen boss.'

'You make me laugh.'

I refused categorically. That evening I was on the list of those who hadn't reached the norm. I didn't try to prove the contrary. Next morning I examined my scarf and took it to the boss.

'Put it through steam.'

'Sure. We weren't born yesterday.'

Happy at this unexpected acquisition, he gave me a 500 gram loaf in exchange.[28]

Or again, one might see at once that a given job, even in

the mine, was the one in which one could survive just that little longer, until some other opportunity arose. One might, for example, become a 'pointist'. 'The "point" is an iron tube which directs a jet of burning vapour to warm the frozen moraine. From time to time the "pointist" extracts the pieces of warmed-up stone with the aid of a pole ten feet long, with a flat metal spoon the size of a hand at its extremity. . . . Volodya no longer needed to think continually, as we all did, of how to find such a warmth. The piercing cold no longer penetrated his being and paralysed the cells of his brain. The jet of vapour saved him. Everyone envied him.'[28]

Another prisoner tells of saving himself when in a very difficult situation by his rusty ability to play the violin, by which he ensured recruitment to the camp orchestra. (These bands, found also in the German concentration camps, were a well-established custom. Solzhenitsyn, it will be remembered, remarks on the farce of the Dalstroy orchestra playing marches and waltzes to the convoy of 'tormented, half-dead' prisoners who, the ships having been unable to penetrate completely the late ice in early May, had to be disembarked on the ice and drag themselves over the last miles to the shore.)[32]

More basically, one relied on 'blat' and 'tufta'. The former indicates influence, protection, the network of gaining favours—normally open only to the *blatniye* (as the *urkas* were also known), though used as far as possible by everyone else who could, particularly by experienced veterans. In spite of the principle of maximum persecution for counter-revolutionaries, there were always cases of commandants who were tugged the other way by the necessity of getting results and keeping things reasonably efficient. If they could do so without attracting attention, commandants under heavy pressure would—in practice if not in form—sometimes use qualified political prisoners.

'Tufta' is the system of faking results of all types. One woman remembers, 'There is tufta in all kinds of work. A man who understands the art of tufta can always turn out satisfactory work, although in reality his work should not pass. In the evening, for example, two wood choppers show their pile of wood to the free brigadier. He checks it and notes down: twelve cubic yards. That is a respectable performance. Nevertheless, the two wood choppers are not noticeably tired. In actuality they have felled just enough wood to camouflage artfully a pile of brush. That is tufta.'[13]

Another woman (Mrs Ginzburg) learnt a practically identical trick:

'You need to keep your heads. Kolyma rests on three foundations: threats, intrigue, and graft. Choose the one you want to star in.'

This was theory. It was Polina Melnikova who showed us how to apply it. She was one of the few to fulfil her norm, yet she worked alone on a one-handed saw. One afternoon we found ourselves working beside her, that is to say we were working, but she, huddled in her rags, had been resting for an hour on a frozen log, her axe and saw thrown aside.

'Look!' said Galya. 'She's like a statue of Gogol.'

'It's true.'

'How can she fulfil her norm sitting about like that?'

We asked her. She said that she had already reached it. Amazed, we pressed her to tell the secret. Looking around furtively, she explained: 'The forest is full of piles of timber cut by our predecessors. No one has ever counted them.'

'But anyone can see that they were cut long ago. By the fact that the cross-sections have grown dark in colour.

'If you saw off the slices at the end of each log it looks as though it had just been cut. Then you re-lay the logs in a different place and there's your norm.'

This dodge, which we called freshening up the sandwich, gave us a respite. We made some variations in Polina's technique. We used as a nucleus of our pile some trees which we had in fact felled. We left two trees cut down but not yet sawn up as a sign of our assiduous activity. Then we dragged along some old logs and after slicing off their ends, added them to our pile.

Of the three foundations of Kolyma, we had opted for the third, and I may say we felt no compunction. I don't know whether Kostik realised why our output had increased; anyway, he never said anything about it.

Our respite was a short one. We had not yet recovered on our full rations from the punishment-cell, when tractors arrived at Kilometre Seven to cart away the timber. In three days all the reserves which helped us to fulfil the norm had vanished.

'Cousin' got into a rage when our output fell to 18 or 20 per cent. We were hoist with our own petard. Again we were condemned to the punishment-cell for sabotage.[4]

More generally, to give the appearance of working, while not actually expending calories, was vital:

During this period of my stay at the Tumanny gold field, the practice of 'conserving one's strength' became a mass characteristic of the prisoners. When there was no official nearby the man at work moved slowly with minimum exertion, halted as frequently as he could to have a smoke, took time to roll his thin cigarette, walked around to look for a match, and so forth. But with an increased number of supervisors, the method of 'conserving strength' underwent a change. Men pretended they were working with great energy, whereas in crushing rocks they put no force in their pickaxes, and in loading wheelbarrows lifted with their spades only half or less of what they were supposed to lift. They moved the wheelbarrows slowly, and often upset them. As you looked from the side, you saw a man pushing a wheelbarrow and apparently straining every effort so that even the veins on his forehead looked swollen. But one glance at the barrow and you saw it less than half filled, light enough for a boy to push. During the time it took the man to wheel his barrow to the panning structure, with a couple of upsets on the way, his two team-mates, who were filling the next barrow, were able to snatch a good rest. This practice had a special name: dimming. You asked a worker. 'Well, how goes it?' He would wink at you and answer, 'All right. Just dimming a little.'

However, the authorities soon began to see through all this, and woe to him who was caught with a half-empty barrow. A resounding cuff on the head sent him, along with his wheelbarrow, flying for several yards off the runway. But this didn't improve matters much. The men realised too clearly that any over-exertion at their exhausting work would soon land them in the brigade for the unfit, with its reduced ration of bread from which it was a straight road to the common grave.[23]

There are various reports of lives depending on small particulars. Several prisoners claim to have survived difficult periods by adding cranberries to their diet. A broken limb might sometimes be better than the alternative: 'Every prisoner welcomes a broken arm or leg—and the bones of sufferers from scurvy break easily. Here, too, the prisoners will assist chance if they have the opportunity. For example they will hold their leg between moving hand-trucks in the mines.'[13]

And we need not neglect the spiritual solaces, which we have already seen so powerfully shown by the persecuted nuns. Shalamov describes an imprisoned priest in his barracks whom he finds at prayer and who explains, 'That gives a little balm to my heart, and then I feel hunger less.' Shalamov adds that everyone had some secret which helped him to live: 'For Zamyatin, it was the liturgy of St John Chrysostom. My secret saviour was poetry. . . .'[28]

All the same, nothing could work in the long run except withdrawal from the irrevocably debilitating toil of the masses of miners and other workers. At the Maldyak mining camp, General Gorbatov recalls,

Soon things started to go badly with me. My legs began to swell and my teeth grew loose in my gums. To lie down sick on the job was bad—there was only ever one result—so I went to see the doctor. He was in fact only a doctor's assistant, sentenced to ten years for some trifle. He was a decent man. He certified me sick, pronounced me fit for light duties only and fixed me up as watchman of the summer water tank. This was considered a privilege; you did not have to push around heavy barrows and trolleys. All you had to do was make sure that no one stole the dry wood for the stoves. I held my rank as watchman for two weeks. I sat in a shelter which I had made out of snow, and kept a small fire going in there. I had a pick and an axe and I used them to hack pieces off tree stumps and drag them into my snow house to keep the fire going.

The work was not hard and inwardly I often thanked the kindly doctor. But my legs went on swelling until they looked like logs and my knees would no longer bend. I had to go back to the doctor. He certified me as completely unfit and wrote a recommendation for my removal from Maldyak to a camp some twelve miles from Magadan. Everything now depended on the camp commander. Fortunately he initialled the document and at the end of March 1940, I found myself near Magadan. This and only this saved me from certain death. I wish I could remember the name of the doctor at Maldyak. I shall be grateful to him for ever.[5]

Then, when he had been transferred:

There were many criminals in our new camp and, as at Maldyak, they worked little and lived well. For a long time one of these individuals had been pestering me to sell him my woollen tunic. He was the senior in one of the tents and drew the bread ration to distribute to the other prisoners, so that he always had surpluses. One day I received a letter from my wife in which she told me that she had sent a parcel containing a new tunic, trousers, underwear, boots and a dry sausage. I showed this letter to the 'trusty'. 'I can't sell you the tunic I'm wearing, but I will let you have the other one when I get it, provided you supply me with extra bread.'

'All right,' he answered, 'I'll let you have a ration of six hundred grams a day.' And, to do him justice, he kept his promise.

From long experience, however, I knew that the good things never got as far as me. Up to now I had never received what my wife had told me she had sent. Some parcels simply failed to arrive. So, not being very hopeful of ever seeing the latest parcel, I felt sure that the extra bread, which was keeping me on my feet, would only be available for a limited time. It was a question of planning a lighter job well ahead. With the help of another prisoner, Gorev, who enjoyed a certain amount of authority, being in charge of part of the workshops, I managed to obtain a job splitting firewood and heating water in the boilers. I was up to this work, and it was warm there.

Next to the boilers stood the camp administration sector where a man called Egorov worked as an accountant. He had once been a finance clerk in Yaroslavl. I got to know him and offered to tidy and sweep his office regularly, in the hope that this might bring the extra crust of bread my way. Egorov agreed—he stood to lose nothing—and I congratulated myself as I swept crusts and crumbs and sometimes even little chunks of bread off the tables into my bag. Now I was able to still my hunger to some extent.

Not far from the place where I worked there were a number of clamps which Egorov looked after, in which were kept potatoes, carrots and onions. I also worked that—hunger is no genteel old lady—picking over the vegetables. I could not chew raw potatoes or carrots whole as my teeth were loose, so I made myself a grater by punching holes with a nail in a piece of tin. Now I was eating raw vegetables my teeth began to strengthen and the swelling of my legs went down. I could even help some of my comrades in misfortune, including my friend Loginov.[5]

In his piece in the Soviet press, Grigory Shelest relates one of the rare occasions when an inspection by the commandant-general did not end in a general distribution of punishments. He describes the amazement of a commandant-general, at an inspection of the *dokhodyagy*, at finding his former army general among them. When he had recovered from his astonishment, the commandant-general ordered the prisoner to be taken to his office, and when he duly appeared, commanded everyone else to leave the room. When the two men were alone, the commandant begged his ex-general to be seated, pressed him to accept cigarettes and offered his sincere apologies. He explained that he could do little to help him (except possibly to make his life a little more bearable), since he, too, was under the sword of Damocles. At the same time he enquired what he could do, within the strict limits of the possible, to lighten his lot. 'You can do nothing', replied the ex-general, 'except perhaps get me the job of store-manager.' This was a privileged position, carrying with it the acquisition of decent clothing and good quality boots. In addition, it assured employment indoors which would enormously increase the old man's chances of survival.

The news of this incident, naturally, spread about the camp and gave rise to a spate of rumours. It was reported, on excellent authority, that the general was a personal friend of Lenin's who had fallen out with Stalin, and that the commandant, as a kind of insurance for the future, had found a means of placing a man so influential (although temporarily under a cloud) under an obligation to him.

Shelest does not hide the other side of the coin, telling how, in the atmosphere created by the event, a Jew named Dodya Shmuller, who was a thorn in the flesh of the authorities on account of his constant complaints and determination to have his 'rights', thought he saw a chance to justify himself. He was, at that time, undergoing a spell in 'Stalin's villa', and existing on the statutory 300 grams of bread per day, and clearly he would not long survive this regime. When the news of the commandant's inspection and its attendant rumours got about, Shmuller lodged one more formal complaint—a desperate one, this time—seeking to prove that the nourishment content of the food he was receiving would not support life. But Shmuller was no ex-general and he received another spell in 'Stalin's villa' for his pains.[29]

Mrs Ginzburg, who was also eventually saved by a doctor after only a few months at Elgen, notes that any claim to medical knowledge was an enormous help.

'When they start filling up your forms, say that before you began studying the arts you did four years' medical training.'

'Why?' I asked, surprised.

'They need nurses here. They will take your medical training into account, and you'll be a nurse, under a roof, instead of having to hoe the ground and fell trees.'

'But it's not true. I'm not competent to be a nurse.'

'Of course you are. Training has no significance here, all the camp women need is a decent humane person. You will be sorry for those who have reached their end and you won't take bribes from them.'

'What about treatment?'

'That's a joke. Here the only treatment consists in one or two days off work!'

'Well, I can't tell lies.'

'Then you had better learn, hadn't you?'[4]

This paid off, as it did in several other cases among our witnesses.

'"But I am not a doctor," I answered in bewilderment.

'"Never mind that," said my friend, "you know how to write a prescription in Latin, don't you?"

'"What have I to do with prescriptions?"

'"You will write something in Latin in front of the chief doctor. This will make a good impression on him."'[31]

By some such method, and given a great deal of luck into the bargain, a small proportion of Kolyma's inmates survived. But it is well to record what a small number they were, what fate faced the majority.

For them the only escape was death. One prisoner reports a great wave of suicide, in September 1938, started by that of a professor of meteorology. But it was always easy to provoke the shot of a guard, and many did. Many, as we saw, were executed or beaten to death or merely killed for fun: one post-war prisoner says,

I was convinced that soldiers of the MVD must have been picked for their sadistic qualities. They had a completely free hand over us and would do anything, particularly when drunk, to make prisoners suffer. For instance, when going to or coming back from work in the usual columns of five, they would sometimes stop us in the middle of the road, unleash their dogs, and laugh uproariously as the dogs sank their fangs into the prisoners' legs. It was a time when they were absolutely free to do anything, even kill us—and get a reward for it. I have known them to call a man over to make a fire for them, or to bring them a mug of water when on sentry duty, and then kill the unfortunate under the pretext that the prisoner had crossed the 'no trespass' line.[31]

Still, the majority died of mere freezing, hunger, polyavitaminosis and exhaustion, or in the routine of camp brutality, by that colder and more calculated violence of the mature Stalinist order. In 1939, one prisoner was allotted to the graveyard detail.

We started out, past the mine, past the punishment shack, uphill to the mound. Our tools were stored in a small booth. A wide square was cleared of snow, and in it two pits were dug, about ten by thirty feet. One of them was shallow, apparently it had been just begun, but the other was finished and already nearly full. Standing at the edge, I saw clearly the outlines of the corpses under the layer of lime. A barrel with lime stood near by, ready for use.

We began to work, drilling vertical holes arranged in chessboard order, in the unfinished pit. When the holes were about three feet deep, they were charged with ammonal and blasted, after which we had to clear away the earth and rock, and drill again. The work proceeded quietly, and slowly. There were no guards about, and the workers were all fine fellows. The blasting was done once every two days. A huge bonfire was always burning near by, and we spent a good half of the working day sitting by it. I fell to talking with the senior grave-digger, a cheerful young man.

'I am a veteran grave-digger,' he told me. 'Even before I came to Tumanny, I buried men at the Berzin mine. The mine was a large one—at that time it employed six or seven thousand prisoners. The camp had to have one grave-digger, and I used my connections to get the job. What a life that was! No worries, no troubles, no control of any kind. The work was easy enough. In 1936 I buried only three men, in 1937, four. What a job! In the summer I picked berries and toasted myself in the sun. The output was always one hundred per cent, the food was fine . . . And though I was not socially preferred, I was considered something of a camp official. The criminals hate to dig graves.'

'And how was it last year? And now?' I asked.

The veteran grave-digger only shrugged his shoulders.

'Now there is almost no difference between working here at grave-digging, and slaving in the mine, except that you are not being pushed around. The work is the same as everywhere else—they drive you to death. Last year there were four of us, then six, and by winter we had fifteen men. Last year we dug more than ten pits.'

'And how many corpses go into one pit?' I asked.

'That depends. As many as it will take. Sometimes thirty, sometimes more.'[23]

The prisoner went on to ask the chief grave-digger,

'"Do they notify the relatives when someone dies?" I asked. "What do you think?"

'"I know that they don't. In the camp they make a record that prisoner so-and-so died of such-and-such an illness and send the information to Magadan, where his name is struck from the lists. If it was a political prisoner, his death is reported to the NKVD in Moscow. And that is the end of it." '23

And, in fact, it was often years before the fact of death could be established by relatives.

Over the gates of the camps in Kolyma there was an inscription required, we are told, by camp statutes: 'Labour is a matter of honour, courage and heroism.' As the Leninist dissident Roy Medvedev comments, this cannot but recall the parallel hypocrisy by which the gates of Nazi concentration camps carried the inscription, '*Arbeit macht frei*'.

The remark which is quoted at the beginning of this chapter, as its epigraph, was made by a French Communist named Derfel. His end, typical enough of many, is described: 'Blows had already come into fashion. One day a brigadier gave Derfel a simple clout in passing, a matter of routine. Derfel fell and didn't get up.'28

CHAPTER SEVEN

WOMEN

> One day Lara went out and did not come back.
> She must have been arrested in the street, as so
> often happened in those days, and she died or
> vanished somewhere, forgotten as a nameless
> number on a list which later was mislaid, in
> one of the innumerable mixed or women's
> concentration camps in the north.
>
> PASTERNAK, *Doctor Zhivago*

THE women of Kolyma shared the general fate. The differences between their condition and that of the male prisoners nevertheless warrant a separate treatment—even though we have already, of course, seen something of women's life in the ships, and in various mixed camps.

The number of women involved is hard to determine. The best estimate is probably around 5–6 per cent—giving about 25,000 when Kolyma held half a million prisoners in all. They served in the farming and fishery camps of the southern coastal area—Talon, Duchka, Yana, Balagannoye, Ola and so forth; in the women's camp at Magadan, which provided much of the menial labour of the capital; at the Elgen camp and its satellites, in the northern area, of which we shall treat later; in various penal camps such as distant Tyenki, which held women *katorzhinki*; and in more scattered camps at Omsuchkan and elsewhere throughout the Kolyma administrations.

We have a disproportionate number of women witnesses—in particular, Elinor Lipper. A former Western Communist who long since renounced the system, she published her account in Switzerland in 1950. Another, Eugenia Ginzburg, was a Soviet Party official who wrote with the intention of publication in the Soviet Union itself, taking the view that 'the great Leninist truth has prevailed in our country and party' following Khrushchev's revelations and attacks on Stalinism; and that now it would be 'possible to tell everyone' about what had happened. Her book was not in fact published in Russia, and first appeared (in Russian) in Italy in 1967, without however getting her into trouble in Russia.

It is truly remarkable how closely these two agree about everything that they report—the moral climate, the rations, the brutality and prostitution. It is even the case that they both served in, and report in virtually the same way, the women's camp at Elgen (though Mrs Ginzburg was there in 1940 and Mrs Lipper in 1943). They are, moreover, confirmed in every essential about this camp by a third account, that of Miss Olitskaya, who was there in 1938.

The reason for the comparatively high survival rate, which gave us the testimony of these and other women, is argued by both these as being due to the greater strength and endurance of their sex. Elinor Lipper remarks: 'Women are far more enduring than men . . . and women are also more adaptable to unaccustomed physical labour.' Mrs Ginzburg agrees:

Men are supposed to be stronger than women, yet somehow they seemed more defenceless and we felt a strong urge of maternal pity towards them. They were so bad at enduring pain—all the women were agreed on this—they didn't know how to wash anything or how to mend their rags in secret as we did our underclothes.

They were the image of our husbands and our brothers, deprived, in circumstances in which they so greatly needed it, of our care.

Someone said, quoting Ehrenburg: 'Poor chap, he has no one to sew a button on.'

Each face reminded me of my husband; my head almost burst from the tension. All of us women were straining, trying to identify our loved ones.[4]

This comes in one of many touching stories of meetings between groups of men and women prisoners, when these have been segregated for long periods. 'Then the men notice the women for the first time. Both sexes flock to the wire. The men and women shouted and stretched out their hands to each other; almost all were weeping openly. "You poor loves, you darlings! Cheer up! Be brave! Be strong!" arose from both sides of the wire. They then threw each other presents across the wire—torn towels, saucepans made out of stolen prison mugs, even bread.'[4]

On the other side of the picture a male prisoner tells of being locked with another group in a barrack, when they realised from voices that there were women the other side of the wall. They knock out a few knot-holes and talk; attempts to kiss cannot quite reach through; finally they induce a girl to take her clothes off. In return they push some tobacco through the hole. One prisoner—a foreigner—was shocked but another told him: 'You're a child, Mike. You expect all women prisoners to behave like Katyusha Maslova, if she ever existed. They are not whores. None of them. They are human, and they suffer as much as these boys do for the want of a word of love and a tender caress. The boys understand them better than you do. They are their own stock, their own blood, their womenfolk.'³¹

The superior capacity of women to survive was of course helped by the fact that they were not used in the gold mines. Yet, as Mrs Lipper points out, 'Strictly speaking, wood chopping is lighter than the work in the gold mines, from which women are exempt. But the transition from working as a stenographer, housewife, or teacher to wood chopping is no joke.'¹³

Moreover, to survive better than the men was no high criterion in Kolyma. The death rate among women who remained at manual labour with Kolyma rations remained high. Mrs Ginzburg recounts several deaths of friends. One 'first went blind, then died in a camp infirmary of a kidney disease brought on by overwork'. Another 'died a month later, three days before a telegram came from her son, emboldened by the fact that he was now an *Izvestia* war correspondent, asking the camp commandant to give her the assistance "necessary to save her life".'Another, 'Nadya Korolyova, returning with her team from the day's work, collapsed on the frozen ground, thereby holding up the rest of the column. The four women who marched in the same rank were angry with her and the guard prodded her lifeless body with his rifle butt, saying: "Stop playing the fool! Get up, I tell you!" He repeated this several times until finally one of the prisoners said: "But she's . . . Can't you see?"' Another, after serving for nearly ten years, was made the scapegoat for a fire that had broken out on the farm, and 'she was threatened with a new trial and a new sentence for arson and sabotage. So, on one of the white nights of the short Kolyma summer, brown-eyed, black-browed Tanya was found dangling from a noose in a hothouse where cucumbers and tomatoes were grown for the camp and farm officials, a swarm of disgusting, fat Kolyma mosquitoes, like tiny bats, swarming and buzzing round her head.'⁴

And in general, as with men, the survivors are those who (as with Lipper and Ginzburg) managed to get 'functions'—in their case as nurses. At a different level, women always had a final resource—their bodies. Mrs Ginzburg sardonically recounts her naive first reaction to the atmosphere of prostitution, when she heard 'a hoarse, alcoholic voice say:

'"Well, what about it? I'll give you a hundred roubles."

'Up till then the question of prostitution had come my way only as a social problem (in connection with unemployment in the U.S.A.) or as an ingredient of drama (Alisa Koonen on the stage; a street lamp in the background and she waiting at one side in the shadow) . . .'[4] And the literature abounds with bread, clothes or cash being obtained by this means. Mrs Ginzburg's eventual team boss was a criminal who would give a pair of warm quilted breeches in payment for sexual interludes. —Even to go sick could be made easier by this method. 'In order to be let off work one had to have a temperature of at least 100.4°. Anything less was scrimshanking. As a rule he used up his quota of exemptions on the common criminals, who repaid him in food acquired from the soldiers or in a more natural fashion, for he, though approaching his fifties, was a lusty male.'[4]

Not that more innocent love-making could be easily arranged without some quid pro quo. At Omsuchkan

Once a week a party of sick men would be sent for X-rays to the women's hospital. Duly bribed, the convict doctor used to send brigade leaders who had sweethearts there instead of those who were really sick. Once in, the men could easily lose themselves among the thousand-odd women and make love at their own peril. Finally, however, the authorities got wind of what went on, punished the doctors, and stopped the illicit visits.

But they were not always so interested in the maintenance of proper moral standards. On one occasion I was present when the camp commandant, Colonel Ponomarenko, asked a brigade leader to paint his office, as well as that of his second in command. The brigade leader said he would quite willingly do the job, provided he were allowed to go over to the women.

The commandant smiled, and said: 'Do the painting first and then we shall see.'

'But I have no paint,' said the brigade leader.

'That's your business.'

'Do I have to steal the stuff from the enterprise I am working for?'

'Did I tell you to steal? But if you want to go to your girl, you paint my office first. I'm not asking you where you get the paint!'[31]

Some women used their bodies more dramatically, for revenge.

One day, looking in mute amazement at all those human ants carrying their heavy loads up the rugged mountain, I couldn't help thinking what an extraordinary picture of human life an intelligent film producer could have made of it. Among the women assigned to this heavy task I recognised a famous young actress I had admired very much when, several months earlier, she had given a performance in our camp at Magadan. I spoke to her the next day. She was Nadiya Milionushkina, winner of the all-Soviet Union contest for drama in 1948. Tall and slender, with thick auburn hair down to her shoulders, beautiful green eyes, and a milky complexion, Nadiya looked like a queen even in the shoddy camp clothes she had to wear. She was arrested in 1949 after being accused of having been the mistress of the German general commanding the Minsk area during the occupation. Her sentence: 25 years' hard labour.

Nadia had been such a distinguished creature in her last camp, her manners so exquisite and her talent so genuine, that not only did *zek* prisoners fall in love with her but even camp officials and not a few *politruks*. She pretended to accept the courtship of the *politruks* until these unsuspecting men invited her to their offices. Then when they tried to make love to her, she would begin to scream, smash windows, bang on doors, and create such a scandalous din that all sorts of curious people immediately arrived on the scene to hear Nadiya cursing the *politruk* for assaulting her. The result was that the *politruks* had to be transferred somewhere else because they had lost face in front of the prisoners.

I asked Milionushkina why she had continued to play such a dangerous game. Her answer was that she wanted to see them disgraced or, more hopefully, shot for misbehaviour.

After she did this several times they revenged themselves by depriving her of her actress status and sent her to this desolate place where she had to carry the daily food rations over the mountain on her frail back. Yet she kept her good looks and remained in high spirits and full of pep. Lifting the heavy bag of food on her shoulders, she smiled at me before taking off and said: 'Believe me, there is nothing more pleasant than to see *chekists* dying to make love to you and then being shot as traitors to their motherland.'[31]

Rape was, of course, regularly practised by *urkas*. A twenty-one-year-old girl about to become a school teacher, but arrested for being of Polish descent and given ten years, was on cleaning duty at the Magadan men's camps. One day, the guard to take her back to the women's camp had not arrived when a brigade of men returned from work. They were, as it happened, *urkas*, and invited her into their barrack where twenty of them raped her. She caught both syphilis and gonorrhea. A prisoner who worked with her comments, 'Her experience was not unique in Kolyma. There was even a common expression for it: "She fell under the trolley".'[13] —One of a score of similar stories on a theme we shall not labour.

As to the female *urkas*, we have already seen them on the

Dzhurma. In Kolyma, they mainly stole. A Polish woman in the Magadan women's camp

appealed to the women commandants here to help me against the apache women and to get me back what they had stolen. Both women were young, in their early twenties, intelligent, energetic, hellishly hard and bad, handsome and extremely well dressed when out of uniform. Their clothes looked as if they might have come from Paris. One of these women got my things back for me but I had better sell them at once, she said. So long as I had them she would not answer for my neck. I sold her a pair of shoes very cheaply (they were worth 500 roubles and I got 180), but it was worth it. By doing so, I got permission from her to buy jam, sugar and gingerbread, and was given work I wished.[2]

One *urka* woman team leader is noted as being particularly praiseworthy since, after in effect commandeering someone's woollen jacket, 'she sometimes puts people on light work for as long as two weeks.'

Rozochki, that is, 'little roses', was the contemptuous name that the *urkas* gave female 'counter-revolutionaries'; female *urkas* called themselves *fiyalochki*, 'violets'. One woman political noted that 'behind the poetic word "rose" lies a rich complex of hatreds for those who differ from the masses.'[13]

The extreme crazedness of the 'violets' marked them out even from their male counterparts. 'One, whom they called Shura, attacked even the commandant with her knife, refusing to go to work. Nothing would make her change her mind. The commandant sentenced her to be shot. Still she did not care. I believe she really did not. Her companions said: "With a character like that, better sooner than later!" I cannot imagine what she thought about, if she ever thought. When I saw her she was sitting on a barrel, her knife in her hand, doing her hair, as sullen and self-engrossed as sin.'[2]

Women were particularly susceptible to brutality and humiliation. One was taken aback when, for the first time, she found in the transit camp that the commander and a couple of soldiers were present at the baths, among hundreds of naked women. Her companions pointed out that they no longer thought of them as human. (This appeared to be true, except for one guard who showed himself keen on a magnificent redhead.)[4]

A similar humiliation is recounted by a male prisoner at Omsuchkan.

Because Guralnik was one of the few privileged people allowed in and out of the camp, he invited me along, on his own responsibility, to the bath-house on 'women's day'.

'I'll show you a scene you'll never see again in your lifetime,' he told me temptingly. I refused to go at first but later succumbed to my morbid curiosity. Dressed in a white gown, and carrying some iodine in a bottle, I followed him into the dressing room which also doubled as a barber shop. Hundreds of naked women in Indian file, heads bowed, silent, had to submit to the indignity of having their hairy parts shaven by a man. It was done once a month. The administration explained that it was for hygienic reasons.

Looking at those women, some almost children, some who could be their grandmothers, lifting one leg up on the bench to ease the barber's job while others waited silently for their turn, I could not help reflecting that even in such barbarous conditions women did not lose their innate shyness. I spoke later to an intellectual Russian woman who spoke fluent English and French and had graduated from Shanghai University. When I expressed my distaste for this debasing practice she told me her own story.

'I was so shocked about it at first that I refused, so they took me by force. Two soldiers kept my hands behind my back, while another two forced my legs apart. The razor cut into my flesh and they had to give it up for the moment, but later they forced me again. Afterwards I had a nervous breakdown and was in the hospital for a while. I thought they had forgotten about me, but they discovered that I was not complying with the mandatory monthly regulation and dragged me out to the bath-house once more. My physical strength was at an end, so I resigned myself to be handled by one man instead of five.'

'Why didn't you ask for a razor to do it yourself?'

She smiled sadly, and said, 'You don't know them. They think that you might use the razor as a weapon. Kill yourself or slash somebody.'[31]

Women were also subject to both arbitrary and 'legal' brutality:

All this time Hala was in terrible pain, and kept begging to be taken to hospital. 'Hospital! We'll give you hospital!' In desperation we invoked the regulations and the 'amnesty' that had been, or was going to be, signed. They laughed again. We had 36 kilometres to cover on foot, with three guards and a dog and apaches. Our way was through the forest . . . with its clear, sharp, northern smell; cones, berries and mushroom-damp, and carpet of soft white moss. . . .

Once or twice we halted to pick berries, for we had been given no food all day. After 10 kilometres like this we could go no further. Hala was writhing with pain. My legs were inflamed, hard, shining, in my hard prison boots; the skin was coming away in strips; blood was running into my boots. Hala was unable to get to her feet. For this they struck her repeatedly in the back with their fists. An insanity of anger swept over me. I began to fight both the guards and their dogs. The rest of the journey was made on a lorry lying among sacks of salt. Hala was taken away from me. Later, in the new camp, called to answer for what I had done, I said: 'The English government and the Polish government will hold you responsible for what you are doing.' For this I was struck in the back with the flat of a bayonet, twice. 'Here,' I was told, 'here is one for your Poland and here is another for your England.' This was on the 27th of August 1941.[2]

On another occasion, at night,

In marched an officer and a few soldiers in their long sheepskin coats, their faces red from the frost and alcohol. They spoke so loudly that everybody awoke. . . . A certain woman patient was to be immediately discharged, given her clothes, and sent back in the dead of night to the camp she belonged to.

The orderly, as politely as he could, replied that he had express orders from the chief surgeon to effect no discharges during the night. He pointed out that in the case involved, the woman ran a high fever and was very ill after a post-birth infection. Removal was certain death.

The drunken officer began cursing him at the top of his voice and called for the poor woman's bundle of clothes. To everyone's horror, the half-dead patient was dressed and, supported by two soldiers, taken from the ward in a dreadful state. Next morning, we heard that she had died during the night in the women's camp.

Dr Goldberg was so furious he refused to take over his duties. He left by car for the district headquarters where he handed in his resignation. As there were very few specialists of his calibre, his defiant attitude paid off. The public attorney came back with the doctor, an enquiry was held, and the officer disappeared from the camp. It was alleged that he was put on trial, but nobody knew what punishment, if any, he received.[31]

A typical punishment for religious believers is reported:

During that mortally dangerous spring, the strength of character displayed by the semi-illiterate 'believers' from Voronezh did much to keep up our morale. Easter fell that year at the end of April and these women, who fulfilled their norm by honest work and on whose output the production of Kilometre Seven was based, asked to be dispensed from work on Easter Day.

'Cousin' refused even to listen to them, though they promised to work three times as hard to make up for the day of rest.

'We don't recognise any religious holidays here, and don't try to convert me. Get out into the forest with the rest and don't be up to any of your tricks. I've wasted too much time as it is making reports about you and bothering the high-ups. I'm capable of handling you myself. If you try any subversion you'll get a punishment you won't forget in a hurry.'

The brute then gave his orders to his underlings. The women refused to leave their quarters, saying that it was a sin to work on Easter Sunday. The guards drove them out with rifle-butts but when they reached the forest the 'believers' made a neat pile of their axes and saws, and sitting down composedly on the frozen logs, started to chant their prayers.

The guards, acting no doubt on 'Cousin's' instructions, ordered them to stand barefooted on one of the ice-bound pools, the surface of which was covered with a thin film of water.[4]

This took place at Elgen, the archetypal women's camp of Kolyma. Outside it was a green-painted wooden arch, with the inscription 'Long live the great Stalin'. Then came a wooden gate with 'Elgen Main Camp. Women's Camp USVITL, NKVD.'

From descriptions of the interior we have one of the clearest pictures available of any camp layout and one worth registering for its typicality. There were two barbed-wire fences outside the camp wall proper, which, itself made of wood, was also topped with barbed wire. At each of its corners was a wooden watchtower manned by guards. The main gate was wide enough for prisoners to be marched in in their usual fives. When it was locked, entrance was through a narrow door which led into the guardroom.

Within the walls was a large parade ground, on which prisoners assembled to be checked and marched off to work. Beyond it, a broad path led between two rows of barracks, five on each side. The first barrack on the left was the dining room (with its connected water-boiling section), then three prisoners' barracks, then the 'club'. On the right-hand side was first a prisoners' barrack, then a barrack half infirmary and half used by prisoners working inside the camp, then two more prisoners' barracks and then the disciplinary barrack. Beyond the left-hand barracks were two latrines, beyond the right hand barracks a closed closet marked 'For free citizens only'.

The next row of buildings on the right consisted of the administration offices with the camp commandant and the labour assignment chief; a barrack for sewing and cobbling work; a shed for the issue of clothing; and the shed with the camp food supplies. Near by was a woodshed and a stable for the oxen needed to haul the water barrows from the stream some way out of camp. On the right side of the entrance to the camp, beyond the guardroom, was the economic office and a rest room for guards. The guards' barrack proper was outside the camp. The prisoners' barracks, each holding about a hundred inmates, were about $65-70 \times 25$ feet. Each had a small entrance hall and a washroom with an iron stove and arrangements for drying wet mittens and foot rags—though, as Mrs Lipper tells us, this was only allowed at night, so that night shifts were not able to dry their stuff out in the daytime.

Mrs Ginzburg describes her arrival:

'I thought Elgen was only for women, but don't some of these people over there look to you like men?'

'Yes, I think so, but it's hard to tell . . .'

At first we made a joke of it. But that's where we had got to. We could no longer tell a man from a woman. As we continued to watch the files of workers passing by, any inclination to joke left us. They were indeed sexless, these creatures in patched breeches, their feet wrapped in torn puttees, their caps pulled low over their eyes, rags covering the lower part of their brick-red frostbitten faces.

This sight appalled us and took away the last remains of our courage. For the first time in many months some women's eyes filled with tears.

So, this was what Elgen had in store for us. We had already lost our professional and party status, our citizenship, our families; were we now to lose our sex as well? From tomorrow onwards we too would belong to this species of strange, unreal beings who were now tramping through the snow towards us.

'Elgen is the Yakut word for "dead",' a woman explained. . . .

Barbed wire, symmetrical watchtowers, creaking gates greedily opening their jaws to swallow us up. Rows of low huts covered with ragged tar-board, a single long lavatory made of planks surrounded by lumps of frozen excrement.[4]

The routine was regular:

In summer the day in Elgen begins at five o'clock, in winter at five-thirty. An iron rod is beaten several times in succession against a dangling length of iron rail, the kind of rail the carts in the gold mines run on . . . everywhere it gives out the same wailing, hateful sound that so tears at one's insides that probably no prisoner ever forgets it for the rest of his life.

At the sound the uniformed women guards are at the side of our cots, pulling the blankets away from us. 'Come on, come on, get up, faster, faster' . . . Then you rush into the washroom where the battle for the foot rags is already in full swing and where you can swear as hard as you like. You find that your footgear, which you carefully tied together in the evening, is now scattered into two different corners and is cold and wet.[13]

Then came the breakfast. First the bread ration, then

the same line forms at the next counter—except that the line has now grown longer by the addition of squads from other barracks. Our breakfast ration ticket is torn off and our drinking cups are filled with a slightly sweetened, faintly tinted, lukewarm liquid, which is supposed to contain the third of an ounce of sugar we are entitled to every day. Then half a herring is slapped down on the counter. Good Lord, are these herrings all head? What has happened to the tail ends? Of course you really know. The cooks have their favourites too, and they can't have everyone for a favourite. The tail end of a herring is almost all edible, except for a tiny portion, while the head amounts to the same in weight, even though so little of it can be eaten. There are quite a few prisoners who save their herring heads, boil them in water and then eat this 'soup'. It cannot be said that they are any the fatter for it, or any the healthier.[13]

The women then form up to go to work;

Once again we line up in rows of five in front of the barrack, and after a suitable wait the guard leads us to the square in front of the gate. There are six or seven hundred women waiting to go out. Every brigade is guarded by at least two male soldiers. The soldiers are not here yet, so the prisoners wait. As yet only the *naryaditsya*, who is responsible for the distribution of work, is on the spot. She is one of the most influential prisoners in the camp, for she makes up the lists of the various labour brigades, although of course she is subordinate to her free superior, the chief of labour allotment. Unlike her superior, she knows every prisoner in the camp, and a casual remark of hers at the right time very frequently determines where a prisoner will be sent to work. She can make proposals for transfer of workers, and since most free camp administrators are notoriously lazy and careless, these proposals are as a rule adopted without question. This applies also to proposed transfers to other and more remote camps. Naturally the *naryaditsya* offers her suggestions on the basis of her personal impressions. To make sure that these personal impressions are good, and in the hope of getting or keeping a better job, the prisoners shamelessly shower presents and flattery upon her. This is the more necessary because she usually is called upon to assist in the daily 'shake-down' or search of the prisoner's person, and she only pretends to search those prisoners who have kept on her good side.[13]

The work consisted of digging, mainly ditches or on the potato fields, and tree-felling. One prisoner asked if, being a trained midwife, she might get suitable work. 'The overseer gave a nasty smile and replied: "There are two tasks for people with your sentence: breaking the soil and felling."'[4] But the digging quota—for the ditches—was particularly hard. It was nine cubic yards a day— impossible even for the strongest women.[13] However, even this was preferable to tree-felling. When Mrs Ginzburg was shown her first tree she asked,

'Do you really think that Galya and I can fell a tree that size?'

From Keyzin, who had not yet left the camp, came the curt reply:

'Not just one. Eight cubic metres a day. That's the norm for the two of you.'

And Kostik, who until then couldn't have cared less about the trees or about us, chimed in, in a revolting boot-licking tone:

'Yes, and you have three days to get your hand in. You'll get full rations for that long. Afterwards it will depend on how much timber you can produce. We can't have any parasites here.'

For three days Galya and I struggled to achieve the impossible. Poor trees, how they must have suffered at being mangled by our inexpert hands. Half-dead ourselves, and completely unskilled, we were in no condition to tackle them. The axe would slip and send showers of chips in our faces. We sawed feverishly, jerkily, mentally accusing each other of clumsiness but we knew we couldn't afford the luxury of a quarrel. The most terrifying moment was when the battered tree began to sway and we had no idea which way it would fall. Once Galya got a hard blow on the head, but the medical orderly refused to put iodine on the wound, remarking:

'That's an old trick. You'd like to be put off work from the start.'[4]

Mrs Lipper recalls,

We would come in, load the logs on our shoulders, and struggle out with them to make a woodpile. Sometimes the weight on my shoulders forced me to my knees two or three times, and each time I remembered a movie I had seen many years before in another life. It had shown Indian elephants at work, kneeling on their forelegs and winding their trunks around a tree, then slowly swaying to their feet. Would I not have been better off if I had been born an elephant?

Then we sat silently side by side at the fire, poking peripheral pieces of wood into the flames and listening to the stillness of the frozen forest crowd tangibly around us. At last the brigadier would appear silently beside us on his snowshoes and call out a loud, genial, 'Home, girls,' as he measured our pile of wood. 'Home', we would repeat bitterly as, accompanied by a single guard, we marched back to camp with the others.[13]

In fact the work was, in effect, impossible without considerable tufta. And even then, as we have said, both women only survived by getting other functions.

Continual failure, or any other crime, like pocketing a potato, led to the punishment cells, and almost inevitably to use of the disciplinary camps of the Elgen complex. For Elgen was surrounded by small subsidiary camps: Forty women, mainly foreigners, at the Kilometre Seven isolation camp near Elgen were guarded by four men and one wolfhound. When the Seventh Kilometre burnt down in 1944, new ones arose at the Tenth and Twelfth. There was another at Kilometre Fourteen, another at Zmeika. But the largest and worst were two described in almost identical terms by Lipper and Ginzburg, in a way well worth reproducing to show the extent of confirmatory detail as between Western accounts of the 1940s and Soviet ones of the 1960s. Mrs Ginzburg asks,

'Was there really a worse place to which one could be

sent from here? It seemed so, for there was Mylga, to which one might be sent from Elgen, and Izvestkovoye, to which one might be sent on from Mylga.'⁴

And Mrs Lipper says,

The outlook for the inmates of the disciplinary barrack was usually shipment to Camp Mylga, which is about 18 miles from Elgen. The conditions at Mylga are so ghastly that Elgen seems a paradise by comparison. But even Mylga is not the last stage, for disciplinary camp Mylga has its own disciplinary camp called Izvyestkovoye, where women work in gypsum quarries. A woman who swings the pickaxe there does not have to reckon out how many more years of imprisonment she faces. She can be quite certain that within a year she will be released from all earthly sorrows.¹³

Another Soviet woman writer, O. L. Sliozberg, is cited by Solzhenitsyn with a passing remark on Mylga: 'At Mylga, when Gavrik was in charge, the punishments for women who did not fulfil the work norms were somewhat milder; just an unheated tent in winter (but one could run out and run round it); and at hay time when the mosquitoes were around—an unprotected twig hut.'³⁰

Into Elgen and Mylga and the other camps there poured a constant stream of women prisoners. For the most part they were counterparts of their male equivalents – 'counter-revolutionaries', *urkas* and so on. There were some special categories—the nuns, for example. Then, a new category of non-politicals came in 1941—

the *ukazniki*. An ukase was issued which provided that any worker who left his job in a war plant, no matter for what reasons, was subject to from six to eight years of imprisonment. Hundreds of young girls between the ages of eighteen and twenty were sent to Kolyma for running away to their villages because they could no longer endure the starvation in the cities where they had been forced to work. Some had only gone back home for a few days to visit a sick mother, but the factory manager would not give them any days off and when they returned they were arrested. They came as adolescents and were instantly transformed by Kolyma into full-fledged prostitutes. Thousands of workers were sent into the Kolyma camps as *ukazniki*, for some petty misdemeanour. These prisoners were given amnesties when the war ended in 1945, but those who had not been physically wrecked were morally shattered.[13]

In 1944–5 came Ukrainian nationalist girls aged from seventeen to twenty-two. One prisoner, though accepting Polish accounts of atrocities committed by the Ukrainians, nevertheless commented: 'But why had Soviet officers, interrogating seventeen-year-old girls, broken the girls' collar-bones and kicked in their ribs with heavy military boots, so that they lay spitting blood in the prison hospitals of Kolyma? Certainly such treatment had not convinced any of them that what they had done was evil. They died with tin medallions of the Virgin on their shattered chests, and with hatred in their eyes.'[13]

On the *Sovlatvia*, in 1949, were a new-style group:

Many of the foreign girls living in Moscow, as well as some Russian girls who had graduated from the Foreign Language Institute, were often recruited by the secret service. Good looks and a certain knowledge of English or French were basic requirements. They would be given the fullest details on young bachelor diplomats newly arrived in Russia and instructed to frequent the Metropol and the National hotels in order to get acquainted with them. Once contact was established, the girls were supposed to use all their wiles and sexual charms to ferret out all possible information pertaining to the affairs of the foreign embassies. All too often, however, the girls fell in love with their diplomats and after confessing their true mission, would implore them to save them and smuggle them out of the country.

Because the 'information' they brought back to their

masters invariably turned out to be inaccurate, those girls
who permitted love to interfere with their spying were
punished with a 10-year sentence. Their crime came under
Article 37, Paragraph 6 of the Soviet Penal Code and they
were designated as 'dangerous social elements'. In simpler
language, they were considered guilty of 'illegal prostitution'. Now, as the ship plowed on, these unhappy girls
were crying their hearts out and cursing the day they had
accepted their assignments. Some of them managed to keep
in their bosoms the tear-stained photos of their former
boyfriends.[31]

This concourse of women of all types inevitably produced
occasional children—though when a *katorzhanka* at Tyenki
became pregnant, soldiers being the only males available,
an abortion (then illegal in the USSR) was carried out by
administrative decision. Pregnancy was automatically a
disciplinary offence, and apart from politicals and *urkas*
'mothers' was the other recognised category at Elgen.

'So that's Mother and Child Welfare!' exclaimed Nina
Gvinyashvili when she saw the first platoon of 'mothers'
surrounded by soldiers with rifles at the ready. But it was
only later that we learned all the details of the children's
section and the joys of motherhood at Elgen. . . .

For some reason, the authorities had decided that Elgen
was an excellent place for prisoners' children of all ages,
who, if they survived, would grow up so tough that even a
bullet wouldn't kill them. As for the 'mothers', this was a
collective term for all female prisoners who had been caught
having an illicit love affair and found to be pregnant. The
regulations concerning them were severe but occasionally
tempered by humanity. Several times a day the command
'Feeding-time' came from the watchtowers, and the
muffled, sexless figures, guarded by warders in sheepskin
jackets, would stumble in ranks of five towards the
children's home. Each woman was given her baby and
faced with the problem of extracting a few drops of milk
from her breast, not an easy task since she was living on

Elgen rations and working on land-improvement. Usually, after a few weeks the doctor reported that lactation had ceased, the woman would be sent back to fell trees or to hay-make, and the baby would have to fight for its life on patent foods. As a result of this system the turnover of 'mothers' was very rapid, their ranks were constantly refilled by the arrival of 'fallen women' from all over Kolyma.[4]

A mother could stay with her child for a week, and was off work for a month. She was not admitted into the children's room, but nursed her baby at intervals in a special visiting room. After nine months the mother had the right to see the baby for two hours a month if she remained at Elgen. However, this permission was withdrawn from May to September on the grounds that prisoners could not be spared from field work.

The children's settlement at Elgen held from 250 to 300 children. Those who survived stayed till they were seven and were then transferred to a state institution at Talon, near the coast.

During their time at Elgen, the children were under the control of, usually, well-disposed but incompetent women criminals, who in any case had no time to do more than the bare essentials of cleaning and feeding them. Toys were hardly seen. 'They rarely smile. They learn to talk late and they never experience affection.' The smaller children forgot their mothers between visits, which always upset the mothers. 'The larger children put their noses to the window and watch knowingly as their convict mothers are marched off in rows of five—behind them the soldier with the fixed bayonet.'[13]

When the children were sent to Talon, it was a strict regulation that the mothers should never see them again. Care was taken that they would never be held in the area, but Elinor Lipper mentions a case of a mother who after various shifts found herself at Talon and was able to get a job as a cleaning woman at the home where her boy lived. She saw him every day but he no longer recognised her. She did not say who she was, for fear of the secret coming out, and was happy enough with the circumstances.

Other special barracks are reported in other women's camps for girls with illegitimate children. The motives many gave for becoming pregnant were that it improved their living conditions a little for a few weeks. At first they were often reluctant to keep their babies, but they were allowed to feed them in the morning and play with them in the evening, and they became attached to them until, at the age of two, the children were dragged away to infant homes.

Even among the lower class of free settlers,

the life expectancy of newborn babies was practically zero. There was absolutely nothing available in those years to feed the infants except mother's milk. But because of the poor food and hard work, most of the mothers were unable to produce enough milk, and the babies died.

The older children didn't fare much better. When we came to Kolyma they were giving hospitalised children one glass of milk with bread and butter daily. No vegetables, no fruit, no vitamins. On rare occasions, such as the 1st of May or some other Soviet holiday, children were given half an apple—green and small.[31]

In general, free women, except of the higher castes, had an unpleasant existence.

A few wives, in the early days, followed their sentenced husbands.

Some women brought from Moscow permission to see their husbands every month if he had exemplary conduct and had executed his norm. But these visits were always in the presence of a camp chief, and the woman never got permission to spend the night with her husband.

The women who came to join their husbands had to cope with the cold and the perpetual changes of residence. The prisoner was constantly being transferred from one place to the other and the wife had to give up her job, found with great difficulty, to follow him to dangerous areas, where she could be raped, robbed, insulted. . . . On arrival she would be exposed to the gross advances of the chiefs and the guards who had taken up the morals of Kolyma. With the female prisoners, there was no subtle courtesy. Undress, lie down and one passed on one's syphilis to her. But to rape a woman prisoner always meant a certain risk. A friend, a subordinate or a superior could denounce you. With prisoners' wives this risk did not exist. Juridically they were independent persons and they were not protected by any law.[28]

But above all, this immensely long journey proved to be useless. The unhappy woman did not get permission to see her husband. Promises for an interview were accompanied by precise propositions. The woman did not find work near the place of detention. If by chance she did manage to, the husband was immediately transferred. This was not a game on the part of the authorities, it was an order. Moscow had foreseen everything:

The wife could not give him food—forbidden by regulations. Have a guard give him the food? It's forbidden. He's afraid to. A chief? All right, but pay with your body. What about money? He has too much, he doesn't know what to do with it. The wife certainly hasn't got the amount necessary, to grease the palms, especially the Kolyma palms. Anyway, there's no way out. . . .

Some got a three-year permit, but caught in this trap they took the first boat back. The strongest—and you needed to have more strength than the prisoners themselves—waited out their time and went back without having seen their husbands. The weakest, obsessed by the persecution of which they had been victims on the 'mainland' and fearing to return there, cashed in on their bodies. They remarried, had children and forgot the prisoner in forgetting themselves.[28].

A woman prisoner, when freed, was in a difficult position. It was impossible to live alone. She would be molested wherever she went, persecuted by employers unless she submitted to them sexually, attacked and raped if out after dark, incessantly importuned. On the other hand, the shortage of women was such that many free men sought out wives, even among prisoners twenty or so years older than themselves.

'I'm off to get a wife,' one former prisoner said, with a light smile. 'A wife—at the fiancée market at the Elgen State Farm. I want to marry.' He came back that same evening with a wife.

Not far from the Elgen State Farm, at the exit of the village, there was a petrol station. . . . Former prisoners would come in the evening in cars and choose a companion. It was the assembly point for newly liberated women. The huts were all around in the bushes. Proposals of marriage were made quickly like everything in Kolyma except the sentences. The cars went off with the newly-weds. The bushes were high and leafy enough for, if necessary, closer acquaintance on the spot.[28]

It was common for a woman to settle with a man, regain her health and looks, and then to cash in on her rarity value with a richer man.

The shortage of women led, soon after the war, to an appeal to young Communist girls to go to Kolyma as voluntary workers. Several hundred applied. They were made the object of a great propaganda exercise. After a short time, however, reports of their heroic actions could only be used in papers outside Kolyma since in the region itself too much was known about what had happened to them. For Kolyma not only killed, it also corrupted. Those who came through whole needed luck, certainly. They also needed extraordinary qualities of personality.

CHAPTER EIGHT

A CLOWNISH INTERLUDE

ONE of the most extraordinary—and disgraceful—things about Kolyma is that its mere existence was ignored or denied in the West over a period of some twenty years. This is, of course, true of the whole labour camp system. But there is the added irony that Kolyma was the one such area actually visited by a prominent delegation of Westerners who managed to see no evil, hear no evil and speak no evil about it.

This Western attitude to Stalin's camp system was not due to lack of evidence. No impenetrable security curtain was required. Individual reports from survivors who had reached the West existed even before the war. Reports by the thousands of Poles who had served in the Kolyma camps themselves, and been permitted to leave the Soviet Union in 1941–3 under the Soviet-Polish Treaty, were soon available. On the basis of these, in 1945, Mora and Zwiernak gave a comprehensive account of the whole system throughout the USSR with special attention to eight great camp clusters under Dalstroy. In 1946, Polish eye-witness stories were collected, with a preface by T. S. Eliot, in *The Dark Side of the Moon*, including a number of experiences from Kolyma. In 1948, the old Mensheviks

D. J. Dallin and Boris I. Nicolaevsky published their classic *Forced Labour in Soviet Russia*, which listed fifteen camps or camp clusters in the Kolyma and gave a long and generally accurate account of the history and conditions of the area. In 1951, Elinor Lipper's *Eleven Years in Soviet Prison Camps* appeared and, in the same year, Vladimir Petrov's *It Happens in Russia*: both of them full and careful descriptions, from the prisoner's point of view, of the Kolyma camps. By now, in fact, dozens of first-hand reports had appeared in the West: and all of them consistent with each other, all of them true.

Over the Stalin period a certain number of accounts of the area were published in the USSR. These were designed to give not only a false, but a totally imaginary picture of Kolyma. Berzin himself provided an Arcadian view in the Moscow press as early as 1935.[25] 'Kolyma—Land of Marvels', by N. Zagorny, a series published in *Izvestia* in 1944,[6] has possibly less relation to reality even than other material published in the Stalin epoch, though 'In The Far North—Kolyma, Indigirka',[21] by S. Boldayev, runs it close.

The accepted legend about the building of Kolyma (as of certain other areas) was that the work had been done by volunteer Young Communists. This theme is strongly pressed by none other than Nikishov in a radio address on the occasion of the 1946 elections in the area;[27] it is more surprising to find the falsehood repeated in *Izvestia* twenty years later,[7] at the height of the Khrushchev interlude—especially as the true story, or part of it, was even then becoming (temporarily) available in other Soviet publications, as we have seen.

For it was at this time, of course, that it became absolutely clear that the accounts given by Dallin, Lipper and the others were completely accurate. Material actually published in the Soviet Union confirmed them in every detail. There were, in particular, the memoirs of General

A. V. Gorbatov, and Grigory Shelest's *Kolyma Notes*. And in addition to what actually passed the Soviet censor and got into print, there was a good deal of *samizdat* material which was published abroad without getting its writers into difficulties at home — in particular Eugenia Ginzburg's *Journey into the Whirlwind*, and the passages on Kolyma in Roy Medvedev's *Let History Judge*.

Readers will have seen how, in earlier chapters, the Soviet material—even the Soviet official material—confirms the earlier stories printed in the West. The ration scales, the locations, names and conditions in the individual camps, the continuous threat of death, the conduct of the authorities towards the common criminals and the conduct of the latter towards the 'politicals', the conditions aboard steamers like the *Dzhurma*—in every way, the earlier accounts and analyses are thoroughly vindicated.

In *The Great Terror*, I gave a number of examples of distinguished Westerners nourishing extravagant delusions about Stalin's Russia. The credulity, stubbornly defended against overwhelming odds in the way of evidence, marked a whole generation of Western left-wingers. Nor, in that book, did I have space for more than a selection. I omitted, for example, Sir Julian Huxley's prize-winning fantasy—that Stalin used personally to go down to the yards to help unload railway trucks. I did not even mention Dr Edith Summerskill's egregious remarks to the effect that Ivan the Terrible was to be remembered primarily for bringing some Western doctors to Russia, as a fact far outweighing any atrocities he may have committed; and that, similarly, Soviet executions were more than counterbalanced by some hospitals she had been shown. (Might it not have been tentatively suggested to her that, even on a strictly medical view, execution could also be held to have a bad effect on the health?)

Nor can we maintain that the final establishment of the facts really ended these delusions. Baroness Wootton, writing in the mid-sixties, recalled her shame when, in the thirties, she went to Russian schools only to be greeted with the cry 'You come from England where they beat children.' The retorts, some of them available even at the time, seem fairly obvious: 'You live in Russia where they beat grown-ups'; 'You live in Russia where they shoot children'; and to complete the story, 'You live in Russia where they beat children—and not only beat, but submit them (as was done to Peter Yakir when he was fourteen or fifteen) to tortures like the strappado, which have not been employed even on adults for several centuries in Britain.'

How was it possible that the clear, cool and consistent material available and published in the West was not believed? What emerges is a sorry tale of self-deception. Few went as far as Jean-Paul Sartre, who argued, in effect, that accounts of the Soviet labour camp system should be suppressed even if true, since otherwise the French working class might become anti-Soviet.

In France, indeed, Kolyma itself was made a public issue in an extraordinarily revealing way, in an exchange in court in the libel suit brought in 1950 by David Rousset, of the Commission contre la Régime Concentrationnaire, against the Communist *Les Lettres Françaises*, which had accused him of falsifying a quotation from the Soviet penal code. A leading Communist defendant, M. Jean Lafitte, was asked, 'If labour camps like those which have been described to us exist at Kolyma, would you agree to condemn them?' Lafitte replied, 'If you were to ask me, "If your mother is a murderer, would you condemn her?" I would reply: "Sir, my mother is my mother and will not be a murderer!"' Similar, if less explicit, processes seem to have taken place in many Western minds.

Perhaps, by now, there are not many people who are

unaware of what happened and what is happening in the Soviet Union. This is certainly a great gain. All the same, the cast of mind which so long and so stubbornly resisted the truth has, all too often, merely turned to more recently totalitarianised countries to project on them its visions of utopia.

Bertrand Russell wrote the preface to one labour camp book, published in 1951,* which concluded with letters from eminent Communists saying 'that no such camps exist'. He commented:

Those who write these letters and those fellow-travellers who allow themselves to believe them share responsibility for the almost unbelievable horrors which are being inflicted upon millions of wretched men and women, slowly done to death by hard labour and starvation in the Arctic cold. Fellow-travellers who refuse to believe the evidence . . . are necessarily people devoid of humanity, for if they had any humanity they would not merely dismiss the evidence, but would take some trouble to look into it.

Such themes are well illustrated by one of the most absurd, and from every point of view, horrifying events in the whole history of the Soviet labour camp system—the short stay in Kolyma of the Vice-President of the United States, Henry A. Wallace, with a group of advisers headed by Professor Owen Lattimore, representing the Office of War Information, in the summer of 1944. It is not quite unique, since in the early thirties there were odd visits by Western figures well disposed to the Soviet regime, like Bernard Shaw, to the timber-producing areas near Archangel. The idea was to refute allegations that the Soviet timber then being dumped in Western markets was produced by slave labour. The method of refutation was the dismantling of the barbed wire and sentries' towers, and the marching of

*A *World Apart* by Gustav Herling

the prisoners into the depths of the forest for a few days, under conditions which can be imagined. This proved effective.

The Wallace–Lattimore visit to Kolyma, though presenting certain parallels, was much more remarkable. For one thing, they were not concerned to refute allegations about slave camps since (as is clear from what they wrote afterwards) no such allegations had ever reached them, or if they had, had been repressed beyond conscious recall. Nor, of course, was the Vice-President of the United States selected by the Soviet government, like those earlier visitors, for its own purposes. For him and his companions, Kolyma was no more than a convenient staging post on their flight from the United States to China; though it was indeed one which, as they saw it, gave them the opportunity, over their three-day stay, to gather useful impressions of the development of this rarely visited area of Soviet Asia.

Both Wallace and Lattimore published enthusiastic accounts. In his book, *Soviet Asia Mission*, Wallace tells us that the gold miners at Kolyma are 'big husky young men who came out to the Far East from European Russia'. He adds that they are 'pioneers of the machine age, builders of cities'. He was much impressed by the horrible Nikishov, who enchanted him when he 'gambolled about enjoying the wonderful air immensely'.

One prisoner comments on this: 'It is too bad that Wallace never saw him "gambolling about" on one of his drunken rages around the prison camps, raining filthy, savage language upon the heads of the exhausted, starving prisoners, having them locked up in solitary confinement for no offense whatsoever, and sending them into the gold mines to work fourteen and sixteen hours a day, at no matter what human cost.'[13]

Of the frightful Goglidze, whom Wallace met later

(describing him as President of the Executive Committee of the Khabarovsk Krai—a nice 'civilian' post—and, more accurately, as 'an intimate friend of Stalin'), he writes, 'Goglidze is a very fine man, very efficient, gentle and understanding with people.'

Nikishov's wife, Gridassova (the commandant of the women's camp at Magadan, of whom the best that can be said is that she did not actually make lampshades out of human skin), also made a splendid impression on Wallace, with her efficiency, maternal solicitude and little un-ostentatious attentions. He was introduced to her at 'an extraordinary exhibit of paintings and embroidery, copies of famous Russian landscapes'. These had been made, Wallace tells us, by a group of local women who gathered during the severe winter to study needlework. Two of the pictures were presented to Wallace by Nikishov. He was unable to tell Wallace who had done them but Wallace later learned that this was typical modesty; for the director of the exhibit told him that they had in fact been done by Gridassova, described as 'one of the art teachers'.

In fact, 'the group of local women' who had produced all the needlework were female prisoners, mainly former nuns, who were able to supplement their meagre rations by doing such work for the Kolyma police élite.

This was a very minor deception, of course. The operation designed to conceal the facts from Wallace and his companions was conceived, however, on a vast scale. The wooden watchtowers which lined the road into Magadan were pulled down. During the three days of the visit no prisoners, who usually provided much of the city's labour force, were let out. Moreover, in case the visitors happened to pass close by, no prisoners were allowed even in the camp yard. Instead, they were kept indoors, and films were played to them over the whole period.

Wallace went to an evening performance at Magadan's

Gorky Theatre. The actors, who were prisoners, were loaded on their trucks and sent back to camp immediately after the performance. And while on this cultural theme, we may note Wallace reporting that 'Mr' Nikishov and his friends also expressed themselves as very pleased with a phoney pro-Soviet Hollywood film called *North Star*, which gave an idyllic picture of life on a Soviet collective farm.

The shops of Magadan had their windows full of Russian products, scraped up from all over the region. For the previous two years there had been very little in these windows, and that mostly of American Lend-Lease origin. One free citizen is reported as slipping into a shop at the same time as Wallace, and buying food which had long since vanished in the ordinary course of events. Another followed—but by now Wallace had left and the citizen was told that the goods were not for sale.

Of conditions in the area, Wallace comments,

The eight-hour day is the legal work day in Soviet Russia. Paid overtime was put in as a wartime necessity. Minors under eighteen worked an eight-hour day, and in the evening attended continuation school free of charge.

These are the actual working conditions we found, and the wage differential of about three to one in favor of Dalstroy seemed real enough, since ration rates at Magadan were the same as in Moscow. Compared to-mine laborers in old Russia, the men in overalls on the Kolyma had many more rubles to spend.[37]

Wallace, whose background was of course agricultural, was taken out to the farm 23 kilometres from Magadan—normally a penal camp. He asked the well-dressed girl swineherds a polite question about their work;which caused some confusion as they were in fact NKVD office staff selected for their looks and smartness and had little knowledge of pigs. However, the interpreter saved the situation.

The party flew from Magadan to Seimchan and then to Berelyakh in the heart of the area of the penal mines. (We have already had occasion to recount prisoners' experiences in Berelyakh.) Wallace describes his visit there:

We were flown north along the Kolyma Road to Berelyakh, where we saw two placer gold mines. The enterprise displayed here was impressive. Development was much more energetic than at Fairbanks, although conditions were more difficult at Berelyakh. Gold, coal, and lead mining are the explanation of nearly everything in the Kolyma region, where there are now about 300,000 persons in the community. More than 1,000 mines are in operation, it was said.[37]

He noted the good clothing issued to the miners:

We were surprised to find the Kolyma gold miners wearing United States rubber boots, because our lend-lease policy had always denied anything requested for gold mining anywhere in the world, including Soviet Russia. 'They were bought for cash in the early days of the war,' Nikishov explained. The miners asked me to take back a message of solidarity to the people of the United States. Their trade union leader, N. I. Adagin, sent his best regards to Sidney Hillman and Philip Murray.[37]

Wallace's comment on camp food is also interesting in its way: 'The delicious fresh Kolyma River fish served us near Berelyakh led me to inquire about the presiding chef of this mining camp.'

Professor Lattimore wrote about the visit in an article which appeared with photographs in the *National Geographic Magazine* for December 1944. After noting the deplorable methods by which Siberia had been colonised in Tsarist times, he went on to celebrate the enlightened system which had replaced them. The 'orderly' development of the Soviet North was controlled by 'a remarkable concern'. This was

Dalstroy, which 'constructs and operates ports, roads and railways, and operates gold mines and municipalities' and which, Lattimore maintained, 'can be roughly compared to a combination of the Hudson Bay Company and the TVA'.

This Soviet development was superior not only to the Tsars' methods, but also to the American-style gold rushes with their 'sin, gin and brawling'. Instead, greenhouses provided tomatoes, cucumbers and even melons, to 'make sure the hardy miners got enough vitamins'.

On this point, a prisoner tells of an energetic and tenacious woman head of a hospital: 'Once she set her mind on something, as, for example, building a greenhouse to raise tomatoes, she would if necessary obtain the glass from Magadan more than 300 miles away. Naturally, a good part of the tomatoes were eaten by herself and her superiors in the camp and public health administrations of the gold-mining region, and very few of the tomatoes reached the patients. But had it not been for her, no patients at all would have received so much as half a tomato.'[13]

No prisoner not in hospital, that is to say no miner, ever did see a tomato or any such luxury. As for the other vitamins on which, according to Lattimore, the miners flourished, we have described the deadly fiasco with the pine-needle broth, which represented the only attempt to provide them. We need only note once again, in this context, that polyavitaminosis is one of the regularly reported causes of death.

Lattimore was equally impressed by the ballet—'high-grade entertainment' on which he approvingly quoted a colleague's remark, that it 'just naturally seems to go with gold, and so does high-powered executive ability'. This latter had certainly been shown. The cover operation had been well conceived and efficiently executed, though one may feel that the visitors failed to exhibit the sharpest critical acuity. Nikishov, who had reason to congratulate himself, made as good an impression on Lattimore as he did on Wallace. He seems to have dropped his rank for the visit, civil status doubtless seeming more appropriate for the idyll Wallace and Lattimore thought they saw. At any rate, Lattimore too, calls him 'Mr Nikishov, the head of Dalstroy', and rejoices that 'he had just been decorated with the Order of Hero of the Soviet Union for his extraordinary achievements'. Even more remarkably, Lattimore felt able to add that 'both he and his wife have a trained and sensitive interest in art and music and also a deep sense of civic responsibility.'[12]

The illustrations to Lattimore's article fully accord with what he writes in it. He was able, for example, to print a photograph of a group of well-clad and physically fit men, taken at a gold mine visited under conditions similar to that at the pig farm. These men bear little physical resemblance to the prisoners normally to be found at the site. The caption is 'They have to be strong to resist winter's rigors'. It is, of course, true that one had to be strong to survive a Kolyma winter. But with the prisoners things worked out the other way. Since they were not expected to withstand its rigours, it was not found necessary to keep them strong.

The present writer had occasion to refer in an earlier book to this absurd interlude in the dreadful tragedy of Kolyma. A reviewer in the *New Statesman* was among those who expressed distaste at the credulousness of Lattimore and the others. In reply, Lattimore found it appropriate to write a letter (*New Statesman*, 18 October 1968) in which he asked, 'Is it assumed that a visit of this kind affords an ideal opportunity to snoop on one's hosts?'

This is, let us say, an odd way of putting it. Accounts were already available about the true situation from Poles who had been released from the area. And even the most polite observer might perhaps have kept his eyes open to see if the sights presented officially were truly inconsistent with those reports. More strikingly, it is difficult to fathom how even the politest foreign visitor felt obliged, after such meagre contact, to insist on the 'deep sense of civic responsibility' of General Nikishov.

Lattimore goes on to comment in his letter that Nikishov 'must have slipped up', since Elinor Lipper 'eventually got out'. The fact that there were survivors is thus used to imply that things were not so bad as they were painted: while if there had been no survivors, no evidence contradicting Lattimore's idyllic picture would have been available. An interesting example of having it both ways.

Lattimore, whose tone throughout is of a levity some might find inappropriate to the subject, adds that 'the cream of the jest' was that the *National Geographic Magazine*, in its conservatism, did not wish him to give publicity to Vice-President Wallace. . . .

A conventional diversion constitutes the nub of Lattimore's self-exculpations. In the original German edition of her book, Elinor Lipper, not having seen them, did not go into Lattimore's and Wallace's writings on the matter. In the English edition she added some—not unnaturally rather critical—remarks. In his *New Statesman* letter Lattimore explains all this quite simply. It was done at the behest of some sinister unknown, as part of the 'McCarthyism' which was then rampant in the United States.

In his old age Lattimore became a hero for the younger sociologists and others in the United States, being lionised at their conventions. His qualifications were twofold; he had opposed American policy, and Senator Joseph McCarthy had falsely accused him of being a leading Soviet spy.

The real evidence of Lattimore's record on Stalinism was that, seldom referred to by himself or his apologists, which appears in the two-volume report of the McCarran Committee hearings on his Institute of Pacific Relations. The evidence was overwhelming that the Institute and its journal were tightly linked to Communist, and specifically to Soviet, circles and that its line was Stalinoid. The left-wing *New Republic*, which had generally defended him, finally concluded (14 July 1952),

The report will, we believe, substantiate these charges: that a Communist Party caucus infiltrated the staff and council of the American IPR before the last war; that IPR officials knew of this infiltration and tolerated it; and that the IPR gave up its objective research function and adopted the role of advocate in China policy. The record will further indicate that Owen Lattimore knowingly accepted these trends and that he erred in professing naiveté or ignorance before the Committee.

For, indeed, Lattimore's role as an apologist for the Soviet regime went back a good way. In his journal *Pacific Affairs* (September 1938) he discussed, for example, the Moscow Trials. Asking himself if they represented 'a triumph for democracy', he answered that the purge of top officials showed the ordinary citizen his power to denounce even them, and concluded, 'that sounds like democracy to me.' (Anyone who could think in this way might, indeed, have found Kolyma admirable even if he had seen it as it was!)

Wallace, before he died, expressed his regret at having so deeply misunderstood the Soviet Union. Lattimore has never done so. It may be that in these cases the more innocent dupes are the ones who do the greatest damage, at least in the short run (which may nevertheless be disastrous). Still, it is hard not to reserve one's harsher condemnation for those who could and should have known better, and for the adulators who later excused them. In any case, even the harshest words are scarcely as painful as the suffering of the victims of Kolyma, so unforgivably misrepresented in this episode. More important yet, a clear and even pitiless account of it may serve to instruct the public—and to discourage potential future offenders.

And there we must leave these special and temporary inhabitants of our region. But what has been said in this chapter is by no means a digression. Granted that this particular case, with Western well-wishers of Stalinism actually brought to the location of some of its largest horrors, is the most extreme example ever to have occurred, it nevertheless demonstrates a major side of Stalin's whole system based (as Pasternak put it) on 'the inhuman power of the lie'. For an important part of his whole scheme was precisely the deception of the West. It is particularly appropriate that in addition to the killers and torturers, and the innocent victims, we should be able to find on the very soil of Kolyma that other key element—the dupes and the apologists.

CHAPTER NINE

THE DEATH ROLL

Cold Auschwitzes of the North ...
YURI GALANSKOV, poet, (died 1972 in
Forced Labour Camp Zh. Kh. 385/17)

As we said in our introduction, Kolyma killed on a vast scale. No official figures have ever been released either about the number transported, or about the numbers dying. A usual broad estimate is that, as the editor of the Paris edition of Shalamov's pieces puts it, the area employed 'depending on the period, from 300,000 to a million "workers"', though the latter figure, for 1950–3, seems on the high side. In any case, as we noted, it is rather less difficult in the case of Kolyma than of any other part of the Soviet labour camp system to arrive at an estimate—above all, because the area was supplied by sea and we have reasonably adequate information about the number of ships involved, their capacity and their frequency.

First, nevertheless, let us consider the problem from the other end, and see what can be deduced in this line from our knowledge of the camps themselves.

We have the names of about 95 camps of all types. We also know of the existence of many more.(For example if to the 66 gold camps in operation in 1940, we add 4 more we know of, which later came into use in the Pestraya Dresva area, that gives us an authenticated minimum total of 70 gold camps, of which we have the names of only just over half, so that there were at least some 30 more besides our 95.)

Thus, all in all we know of the existence of some 125 camps, and if we omit a few which were small penal settlements dependent on labour camps proper, we are left with at any rate no fewer than 100 of substantial size (and a single 'camp' in this usage may include more than one site—Maldyak, for example, had in 1940 four sites, each holding 2500 prisoners in 25 100-men huts). Camps, of course, differed in the numbers they employed, and these numbers also fluctuated for various obvious reasons. We can, however, fairly estimate the normal populations. In the Northern Administration in 1938, we are told that the Partisan mine employed only 3000 prisoners, while such mines as those at Upper At-Urakh and Shturmovoy were regular townships of 12,000 to 15,000 inhabitants; and elsewhere, quite consistently with this, that the average in the area was 6000 to 8000. Similar figures are given throughout the literature.

There is no reason to believe that our register of 125 camps is anything like complete, even as to the areas it covers: for the known figure in a given Administration is often an early one, before later expansion; while we know, for example, that the figures increased in the two years 1938–40 from about 25 mines with some 150,000 prisoners to the 66 mines we have noted with up to 400,000. In addition we know of several areas—Yanstroy, Chaun Gulf, Chukhotsk—in which we cannot specify the names or even the numbers of camps, but which at any rate must have contained not less than 20 more.

At its full development, then, Kolyma must have contained at any rate 120 full-scale camps. Of these at least 80 must have been mining camps proper, with from 2000 to 10,000 inmates, with a probable average of around 5000. The remainder were fishing, agricultural and similar camps of around 1000 inmates each, plus the 80,000-capacity transit camp and the other camps of Magadan itself. Thus, on these rather conservative figures, we reach a total of approximately half a million, four-fifths of them in the mines, in the later period of Kolyma's history.

The figure was of course subject to fluctuation—and especially to increase, as new areas came into operation and new mines opened in the old, though it is also true that some mines were exhausted and closed down—for example, in 1942. From collation of the Polish evidence it appears that in 1940 to 1942 (when the Poles were released) the Kolyma prison population was usually in the range of 300,000 – 400,000. The figure of 300,000 in 1942 is given by a man who worked in the Magadan gold-mining office. Henry Wallace in 1944 was told that the population was 300,000—presumably with about 250,000 of them prisoners. This was certainly near the lowest point and thenceforward there was a continual increase. In general, if (from 1937) we take a figure of 150,000, increasing to 500,000 or more in the post-war expansion, we shall hardly err by exaggeration.

Another—very approximate—approach is to note that the census result for the Magadan province gave a population in 1939 of 172,988 (30,657 urban and 142,331 rural), as against 7580 in 1926. This figure, as always in the census, represents the free population only. If we exclude women, children, free settlers, specialists (such as geologists), port officials and truck drivers, it would seem not unreasonable to think that at any rate not less than some 20,000 of the grand total would have been commandants, guards, and others directly involved in the labour camp system. Estimates from other areas are that the proportion of guards to prisoners was around one to twenty. If this applied to Kolyma (allowing for fewer actual camp guards and more mobile detachments), that would give us a very rough estimate of 400,000 prisoners.

To these population figures we must apply a death rate. There is, of course, no doubt at all that from 1937 the death rate was extremely high. We have noted Roy Medvedev's statement that in the mines, after the war, it was not uncommon for a work force of 2000 or 3000 to be able to send only 100 to the gold-face:[16] the rest, not yet dead indeed, were in the longer or shorter interim condition which led to death—just as we are told that of 3000 *katorga* prisoners sent to the Maxim Gorky mine in 1944 only 500 were healthy enough merely to be transferred to Laso the following year; 800 were incapable, and the rest dead.[13] Again, Shalamov tells us: 'Brigades that began the gold-mining season designated by the names of their brigadiers, at the end of the season did not have a single man left of those who had started, except the brigadier himself, his orderly and some of his personal friends. The rest of the brigade had been replaced several times during the summer. The gold mine steadily cast its waste products into the hospitals, into the so-called convâlescent crews, into invalid settlements, and into common graves.'[28] The survival of the 'brigadiers' reminds us, moreover, that those who did not die included the *urkas*, believed to be some 5 per cent of the total prisoners. If they are deducted and counted as part of the persecutors rather than of the victims, the substantive percentage of prisoner deaths rises proportionately.

Of particular intakes we have some detail. A nurse notes that 'During 1939 and 1940 the hospital swarmed with patients who had been sentenced in 1937 and 1938, while after 1941 it was rare for a prisoner sentenced during those years to show up in the hospitals. It was certainly not because all of them had suddenly stopped getting sick, but because they had meanwhile died in the gold mines.'[13] Another woman prisoner sent to Kolyma in 1938 says flatly that the 'counter-revolutionary' intake of that period was 'practically liquidated' within two years.

We are told, for the labour camp system as a whole, that at this period about a third of the new intake—already physically exhausted, and quite unprepared for heavy manual labour on a minimal ration—died in the first year. In Kolyma, notoriously one of the very worst areas, the proportion must have been higher still—and such is the evidence.

On the other hand a prisoner who worked in one of the camp administrations in 1938 records that the highest figure he heard there for deaths that year, evidently for Kolyma proper only, was 70,000. He takes the then camp population as 250,000, so that 70,000 would amount to 28 per cent, which, though low, is within the probable range. (Another prisoner who worked in the administration gives a 300,000 camp population for 1938, but in any case the figure must have varied through each year, rising in summer, falling in winter.) Figures spoken of officially and even semi-officially may, or may not, be more or less accurate. At any rate, we cannot take them as gospel.

The period 1940–2 can be more easily checked, through the evidence of another category, the Poles, since the survivors were released in 1941–42 after little more than two years, and often less, in Kolyma.

After the Soviet occupation of eastern Poland in October 1939, about 1,060,000 Poles were sent to prisoner-of-war camps, 'forced settlement', or—about 440,000 of them—to labour camps. About 270,000 died in the period up to the release of the survivors two to two and a half years later. Leaving aside special operations against prisoners of war, such as the Katyn massacre, the great majority of these casualties appear to have taken place among the 440,000 who were sent to labour camps. Which is to say, as a general estimate, that about half of these died. This ratio is, of course, for the whole labour camp system throughout the

Soviet Union, most of which did not equal the lethal effects of Kolyma. In Kolyma, therefore, we can certainly assume a higher death rate. And we are in fact told that no Poles at all returned of 3000 sent to the Chukhotsk camps. And in a less extreme area, one notes that at Maldyak, 'In the first two and a half months . . . out of the total of 20 Poles in my group, 16 died. Four, including myself, survived.'[2] At Komsomolets, there were 46 survivors out of 436. By September 1941, 60 per cent of those held in the rather less rigorous camps on the Kolyma River had died.[2]

In all, of 10,000–12,000 Poles sent to Kolyma in 1940 and 1941, 583 survived to return under the amnesty, between October 1941 and July 1942.[17] Even on the best assumptions, this must give a figure of some 75–80 per cent dead per annum. Virtually all the Poles were at hard labour, and it is to that category that the figure must be applied.

In the post-war period, to take a further special case, the Ukrainian nationalists were 'liquidated very quickly'. These were normally under sentence of *katorga*. And here we face a problem. On the whole the *katorga* prisoners were held in distant areas from which, precisely because they all died, we have virtually no reports. We have mentioned the Poles in the Chaun Gulf: and our information on the camps there is virtually nil. Similarly with, for example, the Tyenkino-Detrinsk Administration, where prisoners condemned to special rigour were also concentrated.

This means that direct reports of death rates are from camps which had at·any rate some survivors, so that estimates based on such reports are probably, extraordinary though it may appear, on the low side. Nor do we have any clear idea of the proportion of *katorga* prisoners to others. But at any rate, even in the non-*katorga* mining camps, we regularly hear of a death rate of not less than 20 per cent per annum even in good years (for example in Pestraya Dresva in 1949).[31] The extreme death rate for miners was, of course, brought down when other employees in the mining camps were included, while we must also take into account the non-mining camps, many of them deadly enough, but at least not as bad as the gold areas. If we allow, as all reports imply, an average rate of some 30–35 per cent for miners, we may accept a much-quoted figure of 25 per cent per annum for Kolyma as a rough average, though the total must depend on each year's numbers and conditions.

And now we may turn to the most detailed and substantial part of our evidence, that of the prison ships of the Nagayevo run. We shall not find, needless to say, a complete register of every run with an accompanying bill of lading specifying the numbers of each convict cargo. But we *shall* find, by detective work among the various items of information available, a fairly clear pattern which will pin down within reasonable limits the numbers transported to Kolyma, mainly to their deaths, over our whole period.

We list, in Appendix A, every ship of which we have a report, together with the details obtained from *Lloyd's Register of Shipping*. But, helpful though *Lloyd's Register* is in providing information never previously collated, it is defective in certain respects. The Soviet Union did not make reports on shipping matters, or at any rate not full or adequate ones. This can readily be seen from the fact that the *Dalstroy* is given as having been called *Yagoda* until 1939, whereas the name must have been changed no later than the time of Yagoda's arrest in April 1937. Similarly, the name *Nikolai Yezhov* appears in the *Register* until the late forties, while his name must have been removed when he became a non-person early in 1939: and in fact, the ship is reported by prisoners under the later name *Felix Dzerzhinsky* even before the war.

When we consider our list, the first point to be made is that we may be erring on the side of underestimate. A number of ships are known only by a single report, and there may well be others which no one has named. The first *Indigirka*, for example, is mentioned by a single ex-prisoner and solely in connection with its loss in December 1939, as reported by a survivor eventually sent back to Kolyma. *Lloyd's Register* also reports its wreck at this date, which became known because the survivors were picked up by Japanese ships. But the *Indigirka* had certainly made other voyages that season and possibly earlier, though it is not listed in other accounts of the ships then plying in those waters. (When it comes to the second *Indigirka*, the only reason we are able to list it at all is that on checking the first one in *Lloyd's Register*, we find the second one registered at Nagayevo, which indicates that it was a full-time Dalstroy vessel.) Again, the *Kim* is known only from a single, though highly detailed, report. And the *Kulu*, another Nagayevo register, only appears in the account of the arrival of the May 1938 convoy of which Solzhenitsyn retails an eye-witness report. Our list is probably incomplete: in addition to ships we only know of from the odd report, the Soviet merchant fleet included vessels with such names as *Kolyma* and the *Sovietskaya Gavan* of which nothing is known, but which (on the analogy of the *Kulu*, the *Indigirka*, etc.) presumably operated in the area.

Still, it seems improbable that this deficiency will greatly affect our conclusions. The main and permanent ships of the operating fleet are well known and frequently reported. The ships based on Nagayevo constituted Dalstroy's permanent fleet. There were, as far as our knowledge goes, six of them: and if they were not all under Dalstroy at the same time, we can nevertheless always identify a squadron of four or five. These were supplemented during the Okhotsk navigation season by the ships registered at Nakhodka or Vladivostok, presumably depending on the mutual convenience of the authorities and the demand for cargo space.

The ships used in 1932 during the original mass settlement, the *Svirstroy*, the *Shaturstroy* and the *Volkhovstroy*, are not reported at a later period. In 1933 the *Rabochy* took a cargo of forced labour from Archangel to Ambarchik, at the mouth of the Kolyma River on the Arctic Ocean. Another route, on which the notorious *Dzhurma* first appears in the literature, was the long haul from Vladivostok through the Bering Strait to the same area. Tens of thousands of prisoners were certainly transported thus in convoys led by the icebreaker *Sakhalin*, as also to intermediate camp areas on the route—such as the Chukhotsk peninsula and Pevek on the Chaun Gulf. We have no means of estimating this. And in any case a few scores of thousands of prisoners do not make much difference one way or another to the enormous figures which we can arrive at on the regular routes.

The main route ran, as we have seen, from Vladivostok to the port of Nagayevo: after the outbreak of war in 1941, Vladivostok became a military supply port, and the prison ships were switched to nearby Nakhodka. The voyage led through the Straits of La Pérouse between Hokkaido and what was, until 1945, Japanese Sakhalin. Later an alternative and shorter route came into operation, running, when a railway was established from the main Trans-Siberian line to the sea at that point, from Vanino, just north of Sovietskaya Gavan, to Nagayevo.

We must of course allow for a certain flexibility, to cope with variations both in the supply of prisoners and in the demand from Kolyma. We have indeed seen that the death rate, and the principles producing that death rate, did not vary much. Which means in turn that in the longer run the rate of replacement can never have very greatly diminished; that particularly bad and comparatively good years can be balanced against each other without any great problem. Nevertheless, there were variations. For example, 1942 and 1943 showed a falling-off in the numbers of prisoners—while at the same time, the death rate of those who remained shot up, ration scales becoming tougher, and executions on grounds of 'sabotage' for failure to fulfil the norm being the usual procedure. It is difficult to quantify this. (An estimate of a 70,000 intake in 1942 comes from a German ex-prisoner of war.)[20] The area remained operational, even though the emphasis was to some degree transferred from gold (no longer necessary due to American Lend-Lease) to lead and other products. But the *Dalstroy*, for example, is reported as being taken off the Nagayevo route in 1942 and used to bring military supplies from the United States. By 1944 things returned to the old level. By this time arrests were proceeding on a vast scale in the 'liberated' regions, and the prospect of victory implied that gold would soon again become a major state interest in dealing with the outside world.

After the war the numbers in the labour camp system greatly increased, and by 1950–2 reached their probable maximum, generally believed to be in the region of 12–14 million. This is nearly twice as many as the total in 1940. And there is no reason to think that Kolyma was any exception. On the contrary, following the end of Lend-Lease, gold again became an urgent priority for the regime—in fact more than it had ever been.

Generally speaking, over the whole period, the number of ships on the route seems to have varied from four or five to nine or ten. Solzhenitsyn describes a convoy of four ships arriving at Nagayevo in the spring of 1938,[32] and at least two others are known to have operated that year. Over the period 1937–40 four ships are elsewhere named as continually on the route, only one of which is named in Solzhenitsyn's convoy. In 1940–1, five new ships (together with an additional icebreaker) were provided. We are not able to say precisely how many of these ships operated continuously on the passage.

The numbers carried varied from ship to ship. And the numbers carried on a given ship might vary somewhat from voyage to voyage, partly because those ships might be carrying other cargoes as well; partly because (as with Soviet prison cells) in case of necessity there was always room for more. The *Dzhurma* is reported to have carried not more than 4000 in the spring of 1938, but over 6000 was its *average* load during the same period, going up to 7000 in 1939.

The five ships which came into operation in the latter years are quoted as each carrying about 7000—a figure which is also specified for one of the earlier four. The *Kim* carried only 3000 in 1947, on the last trip of the season; while another ship is reported with only 5000 in 1949. A sailor who served on ships of the Magadan run from 1937 (and again, after being wounded in the war, for eight months in 1942) says that in 1937–40, four ships—usually the *Felix Dzerzhinsky*, the *Dalstroy*, the *Sovlatvia* (after 1940) and the *Dzhurma*—carried 6000 to 9000 prisoners per trip.[33]

It is, of course, not necessarily easy, especially for a prisoner, to estimate the numbers on board. This problem should not, perhaps, be exaggerated: a prisoner ought to achieve a fairly reasonable accuracy in noting the numbers in his own hold and multiplying them by the number of holds (three on the *Dzhurma*). And in some cases, though we have no means of knowing which, the figures were no doubt those being spoken of by crewmen or others. In any case, the range is from about 3000 to about 9000, in ordinary conditions. The figure of 6000 to 9000 given for four of the ships in the immediate pre-war period deserves attention, as it was provided by the sailor who knew the route well. If we omit the 9000 as probably referring to the particularly large *Felix Dzerzhinsky* we might then take 6000 for the *Dzhurma*, the *Dalstroy* and so on.

One prisoner suggests that some 4000 was the most these

larger ships could carry, while the smaller held no more than a few hundred;[24] he was himself, however, transported in 1935 before really intensive shipment of prisoners set in: and the Soviet literature is full of accounts of prisoners who believed that a cell, or a cattle truck, could not possibly hold more than were crammed in at a given moment, only to find the authorities able to double those numbers. Still, if we take 4000 as an average commitment, we are most unlikely to be exaggerating.

The next question is the number of trips per season. This depended on the weather, to some degree. We are told that a convoy arriving on 2 May 1938 from Nagayevo was premature, in that the 50–60-mile belt of ice by the coast had not yet quite melted sufficiently. Other accounts have ships arriving in April. The end of the season is given in several accounts as early December, though the end of November is sometimes mentioned. At any rate, a normal season of 7 months, 30 weeks, or 210 days, was the planned and average period.

On the basis of evidence collated from 62 prisoners, Mora gives the length of the voyage as 'five to thirteen days depending on the type of vessel and the weather'.[17] It would normally be the larger vessels which would take the shorter time, so we should perhaps give an average of seven to eight days for the *Dzhurma* and similar ships, and ten to twelve for lesser members of the flotilla like the *Indigirka*, which seem in any case to have been largely concerned with the transport of supplies. The *Dzhurma* is noted by another source as doing the trip in five days on one occasion,[22] and elsewhere as making the round trip, including unloading at Nagayevo, in fourteen days.[4] On the voyage when the fire broke out (see page 34), which was also very stormy, the Nakhodka – Nagayevo run took it eight days. The *Dalstroy* is also reported taking eight days in May 1940. One estimate is that six days should normally be given for unloading and refuelling for every round voyage; though this often seems to have been less, especially when the proportion of prisoners to other imports was high. Moreover, these figures are almost entirely from the period up to 1942, while in the post-war period turn-around was much speeded up: the new port at Vanino gave extra capacity, while Nagayevo, which initially could handle only one ship at a time, was continually expanded. (The Vanino–Nagayevo run, additionally, was at least a day shorter.) At any rate, a round trip every twenty days for the main prisoner-transports seems reasonably conservative, giving approximately eleven trips a year per vessel. (Our sailor witness speaks of 12–15 voyages a year, employing an average round-trip time of 16–17 days.)[33]

One account gives an impression that, at least in 1940–1, May and July were allotted to the transport of prisoners alone. This would imply maximum loads, and, of course, minimum turn-about time, during these periods, with an estimate of 120,000 sent per year on these trips alone, to say nothing of the other five months of the season.

We know of the occasional diversion of ships from their regular routes: for example, that the *Dzhurma* was once diverted for some days to transport a party further northeast, up the Kolyma coast. Again, there were occasions when the schedule was interrupted more drastically, as when the *Indigirka* was wrecked in 1939; and when the *Dalstroy* was lost when its supply of explosives for the mines blew up at Vanino in 1946.

On the other hand the demands of Kolyma, involving both gold and politics, certainly took preference over the requirements of local day-to-day shipping, and the other ships in the Far East would be at the disposal of the Dalstroy route in an emergency. All the same, it will be in accordance with our cautious attitude in these matters if we make the conservative assumption that on the average the number of ships was 5 and on the average the number of round trips was 10–11 a season.

We thus find ourselves with 5 main ships each carrying an average of 4000 prisoners, and each making 10–11 trips a year, with 200,000–220,000 prisoners being transported annually. (This is an average only, for in 1938, for example, at least 6 ships, with at any rate no fewer than 5000 prisoners each, were in operation—which would mean over 300,000 recruits—consistent with the massive and maximum arrests of that year; and the years following cannot have produced many fewer.) If we now take these reasonably conservative figures, and omit for the moment the years 1932–6, and 1942–3 as cases to be considered separately, in the period from 1937 to 1941 and 1944 to 1953, we reach a figure of 3,150,000 prisoners. If we take the much lower figure of 50,000 per annum for the years up to 1937, and 1942–3, we must then add another 350,000, giving a grand total of 3,500,000. On all the figures we have for labour camp casualties, we can hardly allow more than 500,000 to have survived, and this indeed seems a high estimate. Similarly, if we go by camp population and death rate, take a population of 150,000–400,000 for the years 1937–41, of 200,000–300,000 for 1942–3, and of 300,000–500,000 for 1944–53, and apply to each case death rates ranging from 20 to 35 per cent according to the reported rigours of particular years, we arrive at a death toll of about 3,000,000, after including the lesser casualties of 1933–6. Thus, and it should once again be stressed that this is based on conservative assumptions at every point, we may take it that Kolyma cost 3,000,000 lives.

These figures, though quite clearly within the probable range, are sensitive to the assumptions. Five ships making 12 journeys a year with 5000 prisoners would bring the figure up to 4,000,000. Our sailor witness estimates about 1,500,000 arrivals in 1937–40, which would imply a total of around 5,500,000 for the longer period. (Six ships per annum, with an average of 6000 prisoners and 13 trips per season, would give about 6,000,000.) At any rate, the 3,000,000 figure must be regarded, on the information we have, as unlikely to be exaggerated.

Yet, in principle, it is not a matter of whether Kolyma killed 3 million or more, or even some absolute minimum of $2-2\frac{1}{2}$ million, of the presumed minimum 12,000,000 dead in the labour camps as a whole (any more than it is crucial whether Auschwitz killed a third or a quarter of the victims of the Final Solution). Kolyma still remains the 'pole of cold and cruelty' of the whole phenomenon, the illustration of its essence, and of the moral basis of the system which produced it.

Of the 3 million—or more—dead whose bones now lie in the Kolyma permafrost there is one final point to make. They were, virtually without exception, entirely innocent of the charges brought against them. Indeed, when it came to the lesser sentences of a mere ten years or so, this was more or less recognised, in an oblique way, even at the time. The much-quoted story, recorded by Solzhenitsyn in *The Gulag Archipelago*, of a camp official retorting indignantly to a man serving a 25-year sentence, who had said he had done nothing, that this was nonsense as 'for nothing you only get ten years' is sometimes disbelieved. It is interesting to find an almost identical incident printed in the Soviet press during the Khrushchev era. The writer Boris Dyakov tells in it of how his interrogator said to him 'Prove first that you are 100 per cent crystal pure and you'll get ten years; otherwise—a lump of lead' (*Oktyabr*, no. 7, 1964, p. 82). Similarly a soldier said to Eugenia Ginzburg, 'Of course you're not guilty. Would they have given you ten years if you had been?'[4]

But even those serving 25-year sentences (or those shot) were innocent. In these more serious cases, a few may indeed have committed real offences against the Stalinist order, such as having relatives who had been shot, or having met foreigners, or having served in high positions, or showing lack of enthusiasm for persecuting other innocent people, or the officially listed crime of having 'fallen under suspicion'. But even these were at least innocent, or almost invariably so, of the crimes with which they were actually charged.

Nor should it be accepted for a moment that the frightful happenings of Kolyma were a traditional and typical product of a backward Russia, merely reflecting or repeating the oppressions of Tsarism. From 1938 there were always more prisoners in Kolyma alone, and probably twice as many, as the maximum number ever held in Tsarist prisons of all types throughout Russia (183,949 in 1912). As to executions, more prisoners were executed in the Serpantinka camp alone in the one year 1938 than the total executions throughout the Russian Empire for the whole of the last century of Tsarist rule.

Solzhenitsyn's figures in *The Gulag Archipelago* about executions under Tsarism and communism respectively are from excellent sources. The case in general is so astonishing that there are those who find them hard to credit. But the fact that the figures are of the right type may readily be confirmed from Soviet sources themselves. While a confidential Tsarist document gives 48 executions, for 39 assassinations (including that of Tsar Alexander II) in the period from the 1860s to 1902, the *Small Soviet Encyclopaedia* (first edition) in the article on '*Capital Punishment*', gives 94 in the years 1866–1900. Even if we accept the Soviet figure unreservedly we are clearly in the same range as Solzhenitsyn's estimates, and there is nothing remotely comparable with Leninism or Stalinism.

The *Small Soviet Encyclopaedia*, and similar articles in other Soviet reference books, give larger figures for the period after the 1905 Revolution. This was a time when the Social-Revolutionary Party and the Anarchists were conducting political assassinations on a large scale, causing about 1400 deaths in 1906 and 3000 in 1907. Large areas were put under special regulations, and courts-martial tried those accused of terrorism and rebellion. The Soviet sources give a total of 1139 executions in 1907, and 1340 in 1908; while they speak of 6000 executions in the period 1908–12, alternatively of 11,000 in the period 'following the 1905–7 Revolution'. Accepting these Soviet statistics, and making every allowance for the years not covered before 1905 and after 1912, we arrive at an estimate of about 14,000 executions for the entire period of Tsardom in its last half-century.

More than 4000 assassinations were scored by the forces opposed to the Tsarist state at the height of these reprisals. During the Stalin period one successful assassination is known to have been carried out—that of Kirov—though doubtless there were a few acts of desperation against NKVD officers which have gone unrecorded. No one now believes that Kirov was the victim, in any sense however indirect, of the sufferers in Kolyma.

For let us insist again on a highly relevant fact in comparing these Tsarist and Stalinist statistics: the executions and imprisonments of the earlier period were all of people who had committed some offence—in the case of the executed, assassination or armed rebellion. The victims of Stalinism were entirely innocent even from the Soviet point of view.

The vast death factory of the Kolyma camps is, in fact, to be attributed flatly and directly to the political system which created it. It was, by its sheer scale, by the petty murderousness of such regulations as the banning of felt boots, by its whole attitude and method, more than a mere negative attribute of that system. On the contrary, it *was* that system, carried to its logical end. Kolyma—the threat and actuality of Kolyma—was the way the Soviet government imposed itself on its subjects.

Until this horrible piece of history is openly exposed and denounced by the successors of Stalin it remains a demonstration of the background against which they made their careers, and of the system as a whole. Until they publicly purge themselves of this guilt, until they break with this horror in their past, they remain not only its heirs, but also its accomplices. Some beginning was being made in Khrushchev's time: it has yet to be followed up.

APPENDIX A

SHIPS ON THE KOLYMA RUN

	REPORTED ON ROUTE	EARLIER NAME	BUILT	PORT OF REGISTRY	GROSS TONNAGE	REPORTED PRISONER LOADS	NOTES
Svirstroy	1932	Puget Sound	Tacoma, 1918	Odessa	4768		
Shaturstroy	1932	Aledo	Shooters Island, 1918	Vladivostok	4838		
Volkhovstroy	1932	Galesburg	Shooters Island, 1918	Leningrad	5318		
Dzhurma	1933, 1935, 1938, 1939, 1940, 1949	Brielle	Schiedam, 1921	Nagayevo	6948	3000–4000 (1938) 6–9000 (1937–40)	
Rabochy	1933		Leningrad, 1928	Leningrad	2513		
Dalstroy	1935, 1937–40, 1939, 1946	Yagoda Arnelo	Flushing 1918	Nagayevo	6948	6000–9000 (1937–40) 7000 (1939)	Archangel-Ambarchik Blown up 1946
Nikolai Yezhov later Felix Dzerzhinsky	1937 1938–40	Dominia (cable ship)	Newcastle, 1926	Vladivostok then Nagayevo	9180	6000–9000 (1937–40)	

APPENDIX A (cont.)

	REPORTED ON ROUTE	EARLIER NAME	BUILT	PORT OF REGISTRY	GROSS TONNAGE	REPORTED PRISONER LOADS	NOTES
Kulu	1938	Bioe	Holland, 1917	Nagayevo	6492	3000–4000 (1938)	Wrecked Dec. 1939
Dneprostroy	1938	Dallas	Tacoma, 1918	Vladivostok	4757	3000–4000 (1938)	
Nevastroy	1938	Bellingham	Tacoma, 1918	Odessa	4837	3–4000 (1938)	
Indigirka	1939	Tsinan, etc.	Greenock, 1886	Vladivostok	2336		
Indigirka II		Commercial Quaker, etc.	Manitowoc, 1920	Nagayevo	2960		
Minsk	1940–	Murla, etc.	Flensburg, 1918	Nakhodka	5949	Total 35,000 (1940–1) – average 7000	
Kiev	1940–	Ramschied, etc.	Flensburg, 1917	Odessa	5823		
Igarka	1940–		Teesside, 1936	Vladivostok	2920		
V itski	1940–		Leningrad, 1929	Vladivostok	2336		
Komsomolsk	1940–		Teesside, 1936	Vladivostok	2920		
Sovietskaya Latvia	1940–9	Hercogz Jakob	Malmö, 1926	Nagayevo	4117	6000–9000 (1940) 5000 (1949)	
Kim	1947		Leningrad, 1932	Vladivostok	5114	3000 (1947)	

APPENDIX B

CAMPS AND CAMP GROUPS

	TYPE	ADMINISTRATION	NUMBERS	NOTES
Ambarchik	Fishery	Kolyma River		
Anadyr	Other metals			
Annushka	Gold	Southern		
Arkagala	Coal	? Western		
Arman	Fishery, port work			Incl. women
Atka	Transport			
At-Urakh, Lower (Maxim Gorky)	Gold	Northern	6000–8000	
At-Urakh, Upper	Gold	Northern	12,000–15,000	
At-Uryansk	Gold	Chai-Urya		
Balagannoye	Fishery			Incl. women
Bastoi	Gold	Pestraya Dresva	5000	
Bear Island	Fishery			
Berelyakh	Gold	? Western		
Berlag (Beregovoye Lager)	Transit		1200	Maximum security
Boriskin	Gold	Southern		

234

APPENDIX B (*cont.*)

	TYPE	ADMINISTRATION	NUMBERS	NOTES
Burkhala	Gold			
Butugychlag	Coal			
CHAI URYA ADMINISTRATION			(8 mines 1940)	
CHAUN GULF GROUP	Gold			Penal
Cherno Ozero	Tin, lead;			
CHUKHOTSK CAMPS	Coal, metals			
Debin	Gold			Penal
Dore	Gold			
D-2	Uranium	? Western		
Dukcha	Farming			Women
Duskanya	Gold			Penal
Dzhelgala	Gold			
Elgen (incl. 'Km. 7', 'Km. 14', Zmeika, etc.)	Farming	? Northern		Women
Ferdinand	Gold	Pestraya Dresva	5000	
Galimyy	Gold	Pestraya Dresva		
Gorny	Gold			
Izvestkovoye	Gypsum	? Northern		Women penal

APPENDIX B (*cont.*)

	TYPE	ADMINISTRATION	NUMBERS	NOTES
Kadichka	Gold	Northern	6000–8000	
Khatenakh	Lead			Women penal
Kholodnaya	Farming			Women penal
'Km. 23'				
'Km. 56'				
'Km. 400'				
'Km. 1500'				
KOLYMA RIVER ADMINISTRATION				
Komsomolets	Various		5000 (1940)	
Laso	Gold			
Lobuya		Kolyma River		
Magadan (several camps attached to enterprises, e.g. the shoe factory camp)				
Magadan Transit	General		80,000 +	
Magadan Main Women's	Attached to clothes factory		1200	Women
Magadan Women's		? Northern		Women
Maldyak	Gold		10,000 (1939)	Women

APPENDIX B (*cont.*)

	TYPE	ADMINISTRATION	NUMBERS	NOTES
Marissy Spring				
Matrosova		? Southern		Penal
Nagayevo	Port and fishery			Penal
Nartyzan				
Nechayni	Gold			
NORTHERN ADMINISTRATION			(12 mines 1940)	
NORTH-WESTERN ADMINISTRATION	Gold		(6 mines 1940)	
Novaya Zyryanka	Gold	Kolyma River		
Odinikoy	Gold	Northern		
Ola	Farming			
Olchan	Gold	? North-Western		Women
Omsuchkan	Gold	Pestraya Dresva		
Orotukan	Gold	Southern		
Oymyakon	Gold	? North-Western		
Partisan	Gold	Northern		
PESTRAYA DRESVA ADMINISTRATION			3000	
Polyarny	Gold		(4 mines 1949) 20,000	

APPENDIX B (*cont.*)

	TYPE	ADMINISTRATION	NUMBERS	NOTES
Seimchan (several camps)	Gold, etc.			
Serpantinka	Transport, then execution	Northern		
Shaivinsk	Gold			
Shturmovoy	Gold	Northern	12,000 – 15,000	
SOUTHERN ADMINISTRATION			16 mines 1940	
SOUTH-WESTERN ADMINISTRATION	Gold		8 mines 1940	
Spokoiny	Gold	? North-Western		
Spornoye	Gold	Southern		
Sredne-Kolymsk (several camps)	Gold	Kolyma River		
Srednikan	Gold	Southern		
Susuman	Gold	? Western		Women
Susuman	Farming			
Svistoplyas				
Talon	Farming			Incl. women
Taskan	Electricity	Northern		
Tikhaya	Gold			Penal

APPENDIX B (*cont.*)

	TYPE	ADMINISTRATION	NUMBERS	NOTES
Troloch	Gold	? North-Western		
Tumanny	Gold	Northern		
Tyenki	Gold	Tyenkino-Detrinsk		
TYENKINO-DETRINSK ADMINISTRATION				
Ust-Utur	Gold		4 mines 1940	
Utinyi				
Verkhne Kolymsk (several)		Kolyma River		
Volchok	Gold	? Northern		
Vodopyanov	Gold	Northern		Penal
WESTERN ADMINISTRATION				
Yagodnoy	Transport, then admin.	Transport, then Northern	12 mines 1940	
Yana (on the Okhotsk Sea)	Fishery			
YANSTROY ADMINISTRATION (on the Arctic Ocean)				
Yelgala	Gold			
Ytyryk (several)	Gold			
Yubileiny	Gold			
Zapadnaya	Gold	Pestraya Dresva		
Zarosshy	Gold	Northern	5000	
Zolotisti	Gold			Penal

BIBLIOGRAPHY AND REFERENCES

The superior figures in the text refer to the sources given below. I have not provided page numbers for the books cited, since a number of them have appeared in several editions in various countries; in almost all the cases the material on Kolyma is fairly short, so that anyone wishing to do so will have no difficulty in tracing the original.

1 Dallin, David J., and Nicolaevsky, Boris I., *Forced Labour in Soviet Russia* (New York and London, 1948). Contains a useful general analysis of Kolyma from information then available, including its administrative structure, together with first-hand material about the earliest phase of its establishment.

2 *Dark Side of the Moon, The*. Anonymous, with Introduction by T. S. Eliot (London, 1946). Contains two first-hand accounts by Polish women, pp. 118–21 and 155–64 respectively.

3 Galich, Alexander, *Magadan, samizdat* poem.

4 Ginzburg, Eugenia Semyonovna, *Krutoy Marshrut* (Milan, 1967). English translation, *Journey into the Whirlwind* (London and New York, 1967). First-hand account by a Soviet woman writer.

5 Gorbatov, General A. V., Memoirs, *Novy Mir* (Moscow), March–May 1964. English translation, *Years Off My Life* (London 1964, New York 1965). First-hand account by a Soviet general, later rehabilitated.

6 *Izvestia*, September 1944. Contains a series, 'Kolyma—Land of Marvels', by N. Zagorny.

7 *Izvestia*, 14 July 1964.

8 Karpunich-Braven, Brigade Commander I. S., unpublished manuscript. First-hand account by a Soviet general, quoted in Solzhenitsyn (q.v.).

9 Kravchenko, Victor, *I Chose Justice* (London, 1951). Among evidence given at the Kravchenko trial for libel in Paris in

1949, contains an account by a refugee from the USSR (pp. 265–72).

10 Krevsoun, Ivan. First-hand account of the Berzin period at Kolyma by an ex-prisoner, quoted in Kravchenko (q.v.).

11 *Large Soviet Encyclopaedia* (Bolshaya Sovietskaya Entsiklopediya), 3rd edn., Moscow 1970–.

12 Lattimore, Owen, article in *National Geographic Magazine* no. lxxxvi, December 1944. Account of the visit of the U.S. Vice-Presidential party to Kolyma.

13 Lipper, Elinor, *Elf Jahre in sowjetischen Gefängnissen und Lagern* (Zürich, 1950). English translation, *Eleven Years in Soviet Prison Camps* (London and Chicago, 1951). First-hand account by a Swiss ex-Communist woman prisoner (the English is rather fuller than the original).

14 *Literaturnaya Gazeta*, 4 April 1964. Some notes on inhumanity at Kolyma, published in Moscow during the Khrushchev period.

15 *Lloyd's Register of Shipping*, 1936 to 1956.

16 Medvedev, Roy, *Let History Judge*. English translation (New York 1971; London 1972). Some general material on Kolyma, together with quotations from unpublished manuscripts by first-hand sources.

17 Mora, Silvester (pseudonym of Kasimierz Zamorski), *Kolyma—Gold and Forced Labor in the USSR* (Washington, 1949). General analysis, together with important organisational detail, based on the evidence of 62 Polish prisoners, including one woman (copies of whose affidavits, from the files of the former Polish Embassies in Moscow and Washington, are in the Library of the Hoover Institution, Stanford, California).

18 Mora, Silvester and Zwiernak, Peter, *La Justice Soviététique* (Rome, 1945). Contains two first-hand accounts.

19 *Münchner Illustrierte*, 18 August – 1 September 1951. Evidence taken from former German prisoners of war.

20 *Neue Zeitung, Die*, 18 July–22 July 1950. Articles on Kolyma by a former German prisoner.

21 *Ogonyok*, No. 32, 1946. An article, 'In the Far North—Kolyma, Indigirka', by S. Boldayev.

22 Olitskaya, E., *Moi Vospominaniya* (Frankfurt, 1971). Memoirs, written in 1947, of a former Social-Revolutionary woman prisoner.

23 Petrov, Vladimir, *It Happens in Russia* (London, 1951). Memoirs of a former Soviet prisoner, now in the West. *Soviet Gold*, New York, 1949. The Kolyma material in the above, with further detail.

24 Petrov, Vladimir, manuscript in the Nicolaevsky Archive, Hoover Institution, Stanford, California.

25 *Pravda*, 8 January 1935. Article by E. Berzin.

26 Retts, R. V., unpublished manuscript by a former Soviet prisoner. Quoted in Solzhenitsyn (q.v.).

27 *Russki Golos*, 12 February 1946. Radio talk by Lieutenant-General I. F. Nikishov on 'elections' in the Kolyma area.

28 Shalamov, Varlam, *Kolymskii Napiski*. Unpublished Russian manuscript. French translation, *Récits de Kolyma* (Paris, 1969). Account by a Soviet ex-prisoner.

29 Shelest, Grigory, *Kolymskii Zapisi*, in *Znamya* (Moscow) no. 9, 1963. Account by a Soviet ex-prisoner, published in the USSR during the Khrushchev period.

30 Sliozberg, O. L., unpublished manuscript by a Soviet woman ex-prisoner, quoted in Solzhenitsyn (q.v.).

31 Solomon, Michael, *Magadan* (Toronto, 1971). First-hand account by a Romanian ex-prisoner of the post-war period.

32 Solzhenitsyn, Aleksandr I., *Archipelag Gulag*. English translation *The Gulag Archipelago* (London and New York, 1973–77). Though, as the author says, he has 'almost excluded Kolyma' from the book, it contains a few pages on the area, including first-hand reports.

33 *Sotsialisticheski Vestnik*, 10 December 1945. Interview with a Soviet sailor with long experience on the Nagayevo run.

34 Surovtseva, Nadezhda, unpublished reminiscences of a Soviet woman ex-prisoner, quoted in Solzhenitsyn (q.v.).

35 *Vechernaya Moskva*, 27 December 1949. One of several glowing Soviet accounts of the development of the area.

36 Volgin, V. I., unpublished manuscript by a Soviet ex-prisoner, quoted in Medvedev (q.v.).

37 Wallace, Henry A., *Soviet Asia Mission* (New York, 1945). Account by the then Vice-President of the United States of his visit to the area in 1944. Ghost-written and later apologised for.

38 Wolin, Simon and Slusser, Robert M., *The Soviet Secret Police* (New York, 1957). Contains two first-hand accounts by ex-prisoners.

INDEX